The Origin and Development of Jazz
Readings and Interviews

Otto Werner
Colorado State University

Kendall/Hunt
Publishing Company
Dubuque, Iowa

Printed in the United States of America
10 9 8 7 6 5 4 3 2 1

To my grandchildren: Jennie, Joseph, Kelly and Christopher. May they someday become jazz addicts like Gramps.

Contents

Foreword

The Origin and Development of Jazz has enjoyed enormous success since its release in 1984. Students of jazz have profited by the insights, experiences, and interpretations of Otto Werner, Professor of Music and Bands at Colorado State University. What I admire about Otto is the fact that he remains very active as a performer, scholar, and writer in the field of bands—concert, marching and jazz. To perform, study and write in an area of musical expression help to integrate the diverse and complex phenomena comprising the many different musical forms, but in particular, this thing we have all come to know as jazz. Otto surely has done this with great distinction over the past twenty-six years.

The Origin and Development of Jazz: Readings and Interviews is intended to bring the student closer to the pulse of this modern musical form, as seen through the eyes and ears of those who have had significant influences on shaping its present state.

Through personal interviews with such historic greats as Arthur Duncan, Ed Shaughnessy, Dave Grusin and "Mr. Guitar," Chet Atkins, the book comes alive with stories and personal anecdotes. The sections in The Origin and Development of Jazz: Readings and Interviews parallel the organization of the second edition of Otto's book *The Origin and Development of Jazz*. The reader is therefore able to more fully integrate the significance of each of the developmental movements through the personal reflections of those who "were there" and were a part of the scene when it was happening.

The lists of suggested recordings are a rare composite of important works representing each of the historical periods. Many of these recordings are being re-released by the major recording companies and in some instances are even "up-graded" in tonal quality due to new innovations in the technology of recording (compact disc).

Of particular significance is the section on "Women in Jazz." Otto has presented some exciting developments in terms of very important contributions of women, both vocalists and instrumentalists. This section contains a valuable composite of some of these often neglected historical elements of jazz. Given the more enlightened environment in which to work in recent years, we will continue to see more prominent women performers.

I am particularly delighted to be a part of this effort. In talking with Otto during my interview, much of the nostalgia associated with the big band era took on a new dimension for me, as I contemplated what a book of this nature means for the student seeking an understanding and insight into the field of jazz.

We in the United States have much to be proud of, especially in cultural and scientific fields. Surely, one of the truly significant "American" contributions to the world of music is the development of jazz as both a formal and informal area. We may be importing some raw materials and products from other countries around the world, but one of the prime exports from this great country of ours has to be jazz. Its message has reached around the globe and touched the human spirit of people of every type of cultural heritage. Jazz is an undeniable link to others and something that represents the American energy that has been the driving force of our heritage.

I feel pleased to have been a part of this great development. As I reflect back upon the development of jazz from its beginnings through what I feel was its greatest moments during the peak of the big band era, I have an inner sense of personal pride that my fellow bandleaders and I helped mold the style and direction of our art form. We played for large audiences in theaters, nightclubs, and ballrooms throughout the country. They always enjoyed our music and felt they were a part of it. They supported our efforts and showed their appreciation by coming and listening and dancing. After all, in the beginning this music called jazz was born for dancing, regardless of the time and place. During the big band era, more professional musicians were employed in the hundreds of dance bands than at any other time in the history of jazz. The tragedy is that it came to such an abrupt end at the close of World War II, leaving many fine performers unable to pursue their vocation.

People, places, and events helped develop jazz as we know it today. It has taken many forms and many styles. From the area of Storeyville in New Orleans to the concert stages of Carnegie Hall, jazz and its people have continued to develop new sounds and combinations of sounds for the listener. Who can tell what form jazz will take in the years to come? This book should enhance the reader's curiosity in what might lie ahead. It tells us what has happened and leaves us with a feeling of curiosity about the future.

When, in the twenty-first century, historians chronicle significant trends of our century, jazz is certain to hold a prominent place as a vital communicative direction. It is wonderful that colleges and universities recognize this importance by adding courses about jazz history to their curricula. This new edition by Otto Werner is a valuable contribution to the study of jazz history, and it blends current directions with past achievements. This is the type of book that people can read and enjoy or use as the basis for a detailed study of America's music, jazz. I recommend it to you and know that it will provide interesting and valuable insights into where we have been, where we are now, and where we are going in the field of jazz.

Les Brown,
Bandleader, "The Band of Renown"

Acknowledgments

It is impossible for an individual alone to write a book of this type. With this thought in mind and with the guidance of my editor and many colleagues, I enlisted the advice and help of people considered tops in their fields. I thank the individuals who gave of their valuable time to grant me interviews relative to their careers and jazz in general. Chet Atkins, guitarist; Les Brown, bandleader; Arthur Duncan, dancer; Dave Grusin, composer; Dick Gibson, jazz producer; Ed Shaughnessey, drummer; and Lloyd Ulyate, trombonist. All these men are very active in the music business and are influential in the direction jazz is taking.

Thanks to Reja Steigmeyer of *Rolling Stone* for permission to use the article about Thelonious Monk; to the National Association of Jazz Educators executive director Bill McFarlin for permission to reprint Herb Wong's article on Woody Herman; to Jim Steinblatt of ASCAP for use of photos and the article on the Gershwin Brothers; to Mike Vax for permission to reprint his article on the big bands and to jazz authority Dr. Gene Aitken for the chapter on the name bands with new leaders. I also thank James Warrick for his information about jazz concerts, clinics and festivals and Dr. Carole Makela and Les Brown for their written contributions in the introduction and foreword, respectively.

Also appreciation to Dan Morgenstern of the Institute of Jazz Studies at Rutgers University for again letting me use their priceless photographs. Thanks to each of the following for allowing me to use photographs from their private collections: James Warrick; Ingrid Herman Reese; Tom Cassidy, Artist Management; Dr. Herb Wong; Mike Vax; David Shaner; Les and Stumpy Brown; Ed Shaughnessey; Louis Bellson and Chet Atkins.

Sincere thanks must go to people that have done all the work behind the scenes—Dr. Carole Makela, Professor, Colorado State University for critiques, ideas and editing; Ms. Sharon Sparks for her delicate work in transcribing and editing all the interview tapes; and to daughter Pamela Blue for her typing skills. And last but not least, special thanks must go to dear wife Jeanette for her persistence that I undertake and continue this project. Giving me time off from the everyday chores of horse ranching and keeping body and soul together made it an achievable project.

Introduction

As with many endeavors, what one hears or sees is only a small part of the total. Jazz is more than music, whether that is listening to a compact disc or a live group in concert. As with a painting, a book, a well-tuned car or a prized box of chocolates, it is of interest to ask "what went into this music?" "What are they thinking?" It often has been said that understanding or at least knowing enhances appreciation. Jazz is no different. In *The Origin and Development of Jazz,* Otto Werner used years of experience and study to explain and explore jazz for the reader. He explored this American music form as well as its role as an important cultural and social force in the national scene.

In this book, *Readings and Interviews* he has compiled the views of those intimately involved in jazz performance, teaching, promotion, recording and scholarship to tell their stories and explore their perspectives. Many of these perspectives help explain the evolution of jazz. These people have lived the history of jazz in this century. This evolution includes the forms by which jazz reached audiences in the past and today.

From early funeral bands where the music paid homage to a deceased person and reached those in or witnessing the procession to the electronic technologies of television, and sophisticated recording techniques, jazz now reaches many more people on a daily basis. Air travel allows musicians to put far more miles than hours between performances. Music, technology and business have come together so that some people term today's jazz more an entertainment business than the performance of music. Thus, jazz is a complex and dynamic part of our culture. Studying the music without understanding the broader contexts overlooks the people and their impact on America's development.

In a list in *Fortune Magazine* entitled "100 Products that Make America Best," jazz took a place with 99 other consumer and industrial products (from all-electric plastic injection-molding machines to washing machines and pianos to jet engines). Jazz is unique on the list. It is the only "product" that was not identified with a manufacturer or brand name (i.e. Levi Strauss, Steinway, 3M). Likewise its quality is not as dependent on the platitudes of "managing the technology, the labor force, the managers themselves" to the extent of that of the other products. Jazz is on the list as it similarly relates to the "sales-force bromide: know your customer." There is a better-educated, more cynical buyer out there with little patience for poor quality. He/she wants products that work for the first time and is willing to pay for them. To respond to customers' changing needs and expectations, the manufacturer must be nimble. Substitute the "jazz consumer or listener" for the customer and the message is clear. Jazz has had to change in form and presentation. Chapter III discusses the changes in the Big Bands, one form that has adapted to the "customers" changing demands and lifestyles as well as from the competition of television, movies and recordings which bring the music to the listener, though most often not in person.

As American as we term apple pie and baseball, neither were on the "best" list. That sets jazz apart. Jazz is recognized. It often has its own column in major newspapers, information telephone lines in large cities and a section in the "what is going on where." The pictures and commentary in this book provide perspectives into the personalities of jazz, its performers and entrepreneurs. Many of the pictures and the thoughts of performers that Otto Werner compiled provide very vivid illustrations of how jazz has evolved in the last fifty years. Granted some changes were and still may be seen as negative while others are termed the best thing that has come along. We also may say the same about some of the personalities. This is not negative. We only need to remember that similar doubts as well as praise were expressed by someone about early automobiles and every U.S. president. If jazz had remained as it was in the early 1930s, who would be performing today? Where would they be performing and for whom? Would you be reading this book?

Marilyn Marchall's article in *Ebony,* "Are Blacks Giving Jazz Away?" asked some serious questions. Basically, her view is that jazz is a very important part of Black culture that they may be losing or giving away. If jazz becomes white American culture, it may lose its identity with the Black community. She challenged the Black community to strengthen their appreciation of jazz. Besides the serious questions that she poses for maintaining jazz as Black culture, she encourages the inclusion of jazz in the interests of Blacks. The reader should relate similarly, questioning jazz and other aspects of their own heritage and interests.

In part, the inclusion of a chapter in this book on Women in Jazz does reflect on the heritage of another group. It provides a means of identity for women with those who have established themselves in a field that was not readily made for them. Jazz did not open the door and roll out the red carpet, at least not as nursing or elementary teaching. It took hard work and risks, yet, jazz can be a model for other fields where women still have the door nearly bolted shut to them—major league sports and officiating, the highest offices of this country and administrative positions in many companies and organizations.

Many of the interviews and articles included in this book show how closely jazz, as other music and art forms, is affected by social, political, and economic forces in our society. Some jazz artists have found greater opportunities and acceptance in other countries due to the political and social messages of their songs that were deemed unpopular in the United States. Thelonious Monk had to overcome not only limited acceptance of his style of music by musicians, but also the consequence of being in the wrong place at the wrong time as Robert Palmer describes in his article.

In reading this book in conjunction with *The Origin and Development of Jazz,* ask yourself the following questions?

How much better do I understand an era of jazz, such as minstrelsy or the big bands, by knowing more about the people and their reflections on their careers in jazz during the height of the era? Isn't it exciting to know what they are doing today and what they project for the future?

Often we separate the music from the personalities, forgetting the people. Their daily trials and tribulations have made success a very big challenge. Most of the pictures in the book express the positive side of jazz. The hours of travel, rehearsals, pleading for jobs, trying compositions again and again, overcoming the physical and mental anguish of drugs or alcohol or chronic health conditions often do not show either in the pictures or in the music. Yet it was a very real part of their lives. Many have overcome much to bring us jazz.

How has jazz evolved since you were born? Who was in the spotlight then? Who will you be listening to twenty-five years from now?

As students reading about jazz and/or in a course on jazz, your understanding of jazz is greater than that of most people. Share that knowledge with others to increase their appreciation of jazz as both a music form as well as an important part of Black heritage and a contribution to American culture.

Don't be satisfied with what you read here. Be sure you go to performances of your college jazz groups, those of area high schools and don't miss when the Les Browns or Woody Hermans come to your campus. Be there!

If well known performers or groups do not come to you, look at the entertainment calender of the nearest large city. Watch for the listing of festivals, campus jazz competitions and television programs featuring the personalities and their music. Meanwhile prepare for your tests in class using the study guides and example questions that Mr. Werner has included in the Appendices.

Avid listeners and collectors will find the recordings listed in the Appendices useful in developing their own collections, expanding their listening repertory or challenging friends with "Have you heard_____ recorded by_____?"

Remember jazz is music, people and heritage!

References

Knowlton, Christopher. "What Makes American Best?" *Fortune,* March 28, 1988, 40–54.

Marchall, Marilyn. "Are Blacks Giving Jazz Away?" *Ebony, 43* (February 1988), 90–98. (Includes a quiz to test your Jazz IQ.)

Dr. Carole Makela
Consumer Scientist
Colorado State University

Chapter 1
Happy Feet

Dancing is an inherent part of all cultures. Rhythmic body movements, whether in a form of physical exercise for an individual or as entertainment for an audience, have been known to all societies on all of the continents. Solo and group dancing has entertained kings and peasants, sheiks and tribal commoners. Whether as a ritualistic observance in an African tribe or in the tents of nomads at a desert oasis, the body movements of the dancers have been enjoyed almost to a degree of hypnosis. In some forms of dance, the objective of the dancer was to stimulate and arouse the carnal desires of the audience. This was quite apparent in the performances of the Greek and Turkish dancers, both solo and group, in the palaces of those countries. In these situations, dancing was to entertain royalty and people of extensive financial means. Americans also delved into this form of dance entertainment through the dances of exotic dancers found in nightclubs throughout the country.

Many of the forms and styles of jazz were designed for dancers. Jazz as associated with dancing was an important part of Dixieland and the big band eras. A large portion of rock music is designed for dancing. In both these cases, the dancing is done in pairs. Country western music is adaptable to group dancing such as the cloggers or square dancers. Europeans enjoyed dancing both in the form of pairs and groups.

Dancing has undergone a number of changes in style and execution since its introduction to Americans. The first dances enjoyed were brought from the various countries of Europe and maintained in their original form for generations. Not until jazz music became known and popularized did Americans begin to adapt the ethnic dances of their ancestors to the rhythmic devices and beats found in this new music.

The Africans brought to America as slaves had their own form of dances which they enjoyed during free time on the plantations. The cakewalk, the ring shout and the juba dance were adaptations of the dances that were used in tribal rituals or as personal entertainment in Africa. While a number of the ritualistic dances dealt with some form of tragedy, many were danced as an expression of joy and even frivolity and romance. Men danced for women and women danced for men. Group dancing by men and women together was also common. Regardless of locale, one of the primary objectives of dancers was to stimulate the psyche. Men danced as a means of expressing their virility while women danced as an exhibition of love and passion. This took place among Romans, Greeks, Arabs, Africans, Russians, Spaniards and even the Bohemians long before dancing became popular with Americans.

All forms of the dance must have rhythmic accompaniment. This accompaniment can be in various forms. The slaves used anything available with which to create rhythmic pulses. In some instances when nothing mechanical was available, parts of the body were used to produce a rhythmic sound. This became known as patting juba. It could be finger snapping, foot stomping on a wooden surface, thigh slapping with the open palm or clapping the hands. Wooden or metal strikers upon objects that would create a sharp sound were most often sought. These objects had ideal projection power and could be heard above the singing and chanting that accompanied dancing. In dancing to rock music today, the projection of the accompaniment is of such a high decibel level that dancers cannot sing or talk. During the big band era, some of the bands played with such power and intensity that anyone dancing near the bandstand would in a short period of time have impaired hearing. It was a reaction to the loudness with which many of the bands played that popularized the sweet bands with the dancing public. Hotels that featured dining and dancing as the evening fare hired bands that would play with a dynamic level so that patrons could hold a conversation in a normal voice while dining at a table located near the bandstand. This style of dancing became known as ballroom dancing and included several dances with specific names which, in turn, denoted the tempo of the dance as well as the mood. The fox trot, waltz and jitterbug were very popular during the big band era. The Charleston, named for the city in South Carolina, The Black Bottom, named after the consistency of the soil at the

1

bottom of the Mississippi River near New Orleans, and the Lindy Hop, named after the historic flight of Charles Lindberg were also popular. The rock era with all its diversifications had numerous dances associated with it, beginning with the twist. It also included the boogaloo, the frug, the swim, the monkey, the jerk and for solo dancing the very athletic break dance.

Two excellent movies illustrate the various types of solo dancing found today. The *Cotton Club* and *White Knights* both featured Gregory Hines, one of the nation's leading solo dancers. The second film also includes Mikhail Baryshnikov, noted ballet dancer, who in a television special did an interpretive dance in a jazz vein accompanied by singer Frank Sinatra. Of the many dancers today, performing in musicals, television productions and movies, Arthur Duncan is undoubtedly one of the foremost.

A native of California, Arthur Duncan is best known as a featured performer on the Lawrence Welk weekly television show for fifteen years. Now that the series has ended and is in reruns, he has remained active in musicals and is scheduled to appear in the new movie *Tap,* produced by Gregory Hines. The author became acquainted with Duncan in 1985 when they worked together at the Montana Jazz Festival. The author directed the Montana All-Star Band which accompanied Duncan in his song and dance routines. The production was such a success that it was repeated the following year at the same festival.

Duncan as well as other solo dancers feel that tap dancing is an outgrowth of jazz. It has always been associated with jazz and will continue to maintain its place in entertainment as long as there are forms of jazz. Following is an interview with Duncan on his favorite subject of dancing.

Arthur Duncan Interview

Feb. 11, 1988, Long Beach, California

Q: When did you discover that you had the talent to be a dancer?

Arthur: I really don't know. I guess it was after I'd been into dancing a few years. I started in junior high school in a program I was forced into. I didn't want to do it, but after we did the show, I said, "That is not too bad." So I started taking lessons and soon thereafter I enjoyed it. I never felt I had the talent for it. I just kept doing it.

Q: Who were your idols in dancing, and how did they become your inspiration?

Arthur: Anybody that could dance. I used to see all the musicals that were made into movies. I'd go to the theater in the afternoon and spend the whole day. When I saw a step I liked, I'd go out into the lobby and try it, and then go back into the theater. I'd see the show about four or five times. As for idols, I loved the Nicholas Brothers and the Condes Brothers, and Astaire and Kelly, Ann Miller and Eleanor Powell and, of course, Bill Robinson, the daddy of 'em all.

Q: What process did you follow in order to develop your dancing technique to the point where you found you could do this for your life's vocation?

Arthur: Well, I had two great teachers. The first was Jimmy Mulette, when I was in junior high school. Then I went to a fellow named Willie Covan. I think Willie probably taught every dancer that appeared in movies. Willie must be close to ninety years old, and he's still teaching and coaching dancers. I really never tried to develop any particular style. It just came by watching all the rhythm-type dancers. That's basically what I am, a rhythm dancer. I guess my style just developed from that.

Q: Tell us a bit more about your early career.

Arthur: I was a newsboy, and I got kinda slick! I had a newspaper place that I staked out as my own in front of the United Artists Theater in Pasadena. Around the corner was the Pasadena Playhouse, and Victor Mature and a lot of other movie and theater people would come and buy papers from me. I'd practice my dancing and, when I'd learned the time-step and a break, I'd go into some of the bars nearby, put some money in the jukebox and start dancing. People would throw money at me, and I'd end up making a fistful of coins. I was about fifteen or sixteen at the time, and a cousin of mine who had been involved in music starting taking me around to service organizations and clubs. He got me some bucks for dancing there, and I said, "Gee, you can make money at this!" That opened my eyes. I had no intention of going into show business. I just wanted to make some fast change.

Q. How did you get the opportunity to become a professional dancer?

Arthur: I just kept studying, and people liked the way I danced and would introduce me to influential people. That's how I met Nick Castle, who was very prominent in motion pictures at the time. Nick worked with me very diligently. I guess it was like trying to swim upstream. Nothing came easy. I really had to work hard at it. Nick introduced me to a lot of people. I think one of the highlights of my career was making a tour with Les Brown and being included on one of Bob Hope's Christmas jaunts. I woke up one day and felt that I was right in the middle of show business. I said, "I'll give it a try." At that time, I was also going to Pasadena City College, thinking that I wanted to be a pharmacist. That didn't pan out, so I left school and kept on dancing. I haven't looked back since. I probably should have stayed in school, but I've had a lot of fun along the way. I went to Australia for awhile. I had worked with Billy Eckstine, Johnny Mathis, and Jimmy Rodgers. I went to Europe and stayed three years, coming back in 1963. When I returned, I went to see Sam Lutz, who was Lawrence Welk's business manager, and asked him if I could get on the show.

Q: Was it difficult to get established, or rather reestablished, after so long an absence?

Arthur: Lutz told me the Welk show was a family-oriented show with a set cast and musicians. It was not just a variety show. After about eight weeks I got another call telling me Mr. Welk wanted to put me on as a guest. I went on the show as a guest, and then another eight weeks passed and he had me on again. This went on for about eight months when Lawrence asked me to go along to Lake Tahoe to work at Harrah's Casino and Hotel. On the last night of the engagement, after I finished a couple of numbers, he called me back on stage and said, "You know, Arthur, the people seem to like you, so I think I'll make you a permanent member of the Lawrence Welk family." That's how he hired me.

Gershwin poster

Q: How were you programmed into the format of the show? Did you appear as a featured member of the cast each week?

Arthur: Lawrence liked dancing, so he featured me every week. Then there were occasions when I worked with Bobby Burgess and Jack Imel. The three of us would dance the really hot numbers. Lawrence liked that. He wanted to hear a lot of taps.

Q: In other words, you "pre-tapped" it?

Arthur: Yeah, just like singers lip sync a vocal. You had to go out and remember what you'd recorded earlier. I kept it pretty basic.

Q: Did you know the musical arrangement ahead of time?

Arthur: I had to do everything by numbers of measures. Sometimes they felt a song didn't fit, so they would rearrange it for me; play the first chorus, establish the melody, then break it up into fours—four bars for the band, four bars for me. I had to be able to do that on a moment's notice. I'd go into a coat room and work out my taps by the number of bars given to me. They'd call me out when they were ready to tape, whether I was ready or not. Lots of pressure! Your job was always hangin' by a thread. I don't think Lawrence and the other directors and producers really understood my plight. I got help from every dancer in town.

Q: Who was responsible for the selection of the music you used?

Arthur: It all came down to Lawrence. We could make recommendations and suggestions of songs, but if it didn't fit in with a particular theme, it would be changed, and sometimes we didn't know of the changes until recording day.

Q: When you work up a new routine, what is your procedure for determining length, type of music, and dance style to be used?

Arthur: You think in terms of the song. If it's something slow like "Tea for Two," you automatically think in terms of a soft-shoe routine. If it's a waltz clog, like "The Daughter of Rosie O'Grady," or something with a jazz waltz feel, you structure the steps so they are easily identified. I guess I'm trying to say "simplicity."

Q: When and where did tap dancing originate?

Arthur: Geographically, I believe in New Orleans, along with the beginnings of jazz. Guys would dance on the street corners while the instrumentalists would play their early forms of jazz. From there, it became a part of the minstrel shows, and from there to vaudeville, and finally to the Broadway musicals and motion pictures.

Q: Has tap dancing changed much during the various eras of jazz, from minstrel shows through musicals and movies?

Arthur: Everything is very basic. I think it's in the presentation. It's become much more refined, more classical. Fred Astaire was more a ballroom-style dancer, while Gene Kelly was a hoofer who incorporated a little ballet and a little jazz. The Nicholas Brothers were very athletic. They'd run up the side of a wall, do a flip and drop and do splits. I would just cringe when I saw that.

Q: You indicate that tap dancing is a physical art form. How do you compare the physical requirements of tap dancing with other dance styles such as ballet, modern, jazz and Latin?

Arthur: They are all extremely physical and all are equally taxing. Ballet may perhaps be the most demanding of the body to execute. Ballet pulls the body to the "nth" degree. But then, they are all very strenuous.

Q: Tap dancing, like drumming, requires the performer to execute a certain number of taps per beat. In developing a routine, do you predetermine the exact number of taps per beat that you will use?

Arthur: I've never really thought of it in that manner. I establish a pattern in the dance. My steps are constructed basically as an eight-bar step or a six-bar step with a two-bar break. The correlation between drumming and tap dancing is interesting. Buddy Rich, one of the world's foremost jazz drummers, was also a tremendous dancer. He got into show business at a very early age as a dancer, before he was big enough to play the drums.

Q: There are not many professional tap dancers today. What do you feel is the reason for the decline in their numbers?

Arthur: There are not the theaters or the nightclubs that were around thirty-five or forty years ago. After vaudeville, entertainment moved into the nightclubs. When the nightclubs diminished, the dancers had to find other means to support their families. Many are still around, but doing other things.

Q: What effect has television had on your profession?

Arthur: Television has had a positive effect, and, of course, the remake of many of the musicals. Take this show I'm rehearsing now, Gershwin's *My One and Only.* It's all hoofing. All those people in it are doing some really heavy hoofing. I feel everything runs in cycles. I think for the next ten or fifteen years, you're going to see a lot of hoofing by a large number of great dancers. I hope I live long enough to be a part of it.

Q: You have a full performance schedule at this time. What are some of the noteworthy experiences you've had on the road?

Arthur: When I worked for Home Savings, we would tour the country opening new offices. I worked with the same group of musicians, all of whom knew my music. There were no production and rehearsal problems. However, in the days of what we call the "learning curve," matters were quite different. It was during the lean years. Things weren't going very well for me. I'd go into clubs and see if I could talk the manager into giving me a gig. I'd go out and do a number as an audition. On one particular night, I went into a club with my musical arrangements tucked under my arm, only to find out that the only musician on the band that could read music was the drummer! Somehow, we put something together and I got up and danced, and sure enough, I got the gig! You know, sometimes you go in and have a show planned, and for some reason you're not able to do what you want, so you just improvise, and that comes from experience and paying an awful lot of dues.

Q: If you could do things over, would you change the course of your life, or do what you're doing?

Arthur: I should have listened to my mother and stayed in school. No, not really. I wouldn't change a thing.

Q: What personal satisfaction do you get from performing for the public?

Arthur: I enjoy what I'm doing, and I get satisfaction from seeing other people enjoy what I'm doing. That stimulates me, being able to entertain people by doing something that someone else enjoys watching.

Q: What advice do you have for someone wanting to make a career out of dancing?

Arthur: The first thing is to learn to cope with rejection. They'll have their share of that. They must have "stick-a-bility." They must be able to hang in there, to persevere. They need to make up their minds that it's going to be awfully hard physical and mental work. Condition themselves. Learn everything about the art that they can. Unfortunately, they may be the best performer for the part, but if the producer's friend wants the gig, you know who is going to get it. It's unfortunate, but sometimes these are the breaks. But, first and foremost, learn your craft. Develop your skills and talents.

Q: Arthur, how do you spend your leisure time?

Arthur: Lookin' for work! I used to play a little tennis, but I fell one time and nearly ruined my career, so I don't do that anymore. I can't afford that type of luxury. Dancing is my bread and butter. I do enjoy watching other performers. I also enjoy spending time with show people talking show talk. That's stimulating.

Q: What goals do you still have for your career?

Arthur: I've always wanted to do musical comedy. I'm very fortunate to have a feature spot in this musical, *My One and Only*. The director is terrific. I also would like to be able to stage musical comedy. I'm learning that end of the business and find it is totally different from the other end, that of a performer, but I wouldn't want to give up that aspect of it. I'd also like to become a theater performer. I'd still have to do nightclubs and occasional one-nighters. I feel I'm still learning my craft. You know, with each new gig, you almost have to start at square one again.

The Author (left) with Arthur Duncan between rehearsals during the 1985 Montana Jazz Festival.

Chapter 2
Composers

Ziegfield Follies poster

Jazz has given birth to the composition of music throughout all its eras. The work song produced songs relating to the lives of the slaves on the plantations. Many of these songs have found their place in the library of songs of and about America. Stephen Foster wrote music for minstrel shows, designed to elicit various audience reactions from sorrow to joy to humor. Many of his songs are categorized as examples of our early folk music. Men such as Scott Joplin familiarized the nation with the style of ragtime, while the Gershwin brothers, George and Ira, gave the nation some of our finest songs. Thelonious Monk, a pianist by reputation during the cool period in jazz, also had a talent for composition. His ''Round Midnight'' has become a classic among jazz musicians and was recently made into a movie titled 'Round Midnight featuring saxophonist Dexter Gordon. The lives of these composers provide an interesting insight into the lives of all composers. Not everything they write will become a hit. Irving Berlin lamented the fact that he had a two-year period in which nothing he wrote became a "hit." This became so depressing that he considered abandoning composition and changing vocations.

Here are three articles about some of our best known composers. Each composer had separate methods, styles and objectives for his music.

American Classics
George and Ira Gershwin

Edward Jablonski

Ira (left) and George Gershwin (Courtesy of ASCAP, Ed Jablonski).

An old anecdote has George Gershwin in his favorite spot, at the piano. He had just finished playing an extended medley of his songs. In the brief hush that invariably followed his performances, he was heard to muse, "I wonder if my music will be played a hundred years from now."

"Yes," quipped his friend Newman Levy, "if you're around to play it."

It is a snappy Jazz Age retort. Still, half that time has passed since the composer's death at the age of 38—and his music is heard more than ever. No doubt it will be played a hundred years from now.

George Gershwin was born in Brooklyn on September 26, 1898. Six weeks later the family was back in Manhattan, where his brother, Ira, had been born on December 6, 1896. It was there that the brothers grew up, learned their respective trades, and would make musical history.

The Gershwin collaboration was unique—and inevitable, not because they shared the same quarters for virtually all of their professional lives, but because their talents were singularly attuned and complementary. Yet as personalities they were opposites: George was dynamic, quick-moving, gregarious: Ira phlegmatic, a slow-working polisher and a homebody.

As a boy Ira was bookish, his tastes running from dime novels through A. Conan Doyle to the classics. George was not. He did his running in the streets, roller skated (champion of Seventh Street on the Lower

East Side), and skipped school. When an interviewer asked, "Didn't you play anything when you were a youngster?" the answer was, "Yes. Hooky."

George's initial study of the piano began at the ripe age of 12. Three years later he took a job playing in Tin Pin Alley, where music publishers would hawk their wares to performers and sheet-music retailers. There his desire to compose was nurtured, inspired by the suave melodies of Jerome Kern and the earthy rhythms of Irving Berlin, as well as the music he heard in concert and recital halls. He would begin to fuse these two worlds and eventually create his own signature. By the time he was 20, George had written a number of solo piano "novelettes" as well as a *Lullaby* for string quartet, and had filled several "tune books" with ideas for songs and instrumentals.

Ira's progress was synchronous, though still bookish. He attended Townsend Harris Hall for exceptional students. There he attracted attention as an artist and contributed drawings to the *Academic Herald,* the school paper on which he served as an art editor. He also collaborated on a column, "Much Ado," with a Lower East Side friend, Isidore Hochberg (later to be better known as lyricist E. Y. "Yip" Harburg). Ira's later mentor was the renowned satirist P. G. Wodehouse, one of Kern's early lyricists.

The outpouring of inspired songs from George began with the innocuous through charming "When You Want 'Em You Can't Get 'Em, When You've Got 'Em You Don't Want 'Em" (lyric by Murray Roth), his first published song, written when he was about 17. Just four years later, in 1919, George took a giant step with "Swanee" (lyric by Irving Caesar), which led to his being hired to write for a series of revues, the *George White Scandals.*

The Gershwin collection began in earnest when the brothers managed to place a song, "The Real American Folk Song (Is a Rag)," in *Ladies First* (1918). (Ira was then known as "Arthur Francis," because he did not want to make his way into the business on his brother's name. The pen name was concocted from the names of their younger brother and sister.) Contrary to legend, George brought a solid musical background to his work, whether applied to a 32-bar song or a half-hour concerto. Ira too worked from a near academic base. While rejecting the idea that a lyric was a poem, he labored over his words as if it were. The wry wit, adroit rhymes, the often arresting and unexpected but right word, all of which seems so true and so effortless—were the result of hard work.

George's creations—melodies, rhythms that frequently laughed, and harmonies that enriched those spare melodies—came easier, although he admitted that making music could be "nerve-racking" and "mentally arduous." He had technique to burn, but he relied as much on instinct—"ideas" and "feeling" were most important to him; no one could have taught him to do what he did.

The Gershwin brothers hit their stride in 1924 with the epochal *Lady, Be Good!,* one of the earliest of what were called "smart" shows at the time, a turning away from European operetta and toward more modern American themes and settings, with songs to match: "Fascinating Rhythm," the title song, and the torch classic "The Man I Love." The show's pace was swift; it was urbane and funny. And it started a great team, Fred and Adele Astaire, in their first American smash. Incidentally, while the book was merest fluff, many of the songs were "integrated" into it—a rare occurrence at the time. *Lady* set the tone for most of the Gershwin musicals throughout the Twenties and into the Thirties. The music was sophisticated, unsentimental. (Not that the Gershwins ignored the romantic ballad. They merely approached it differently, with tongue, often, in cheek.) The scores that followed produced more of the same: *Oh, Kay!* 1926; ("Someone to Watch Over Me," "Clap Yo' Hands, "Do, Do, Do") and *Funny Face* 1927; (" 'S Wonderful," "My One and Only," "How Long Has This Been Going On?"). *Strike Up the Band* was the first of the three political operettas and marked their transition away from the 1920's musical comedy. A great success, it produced such standards as the title song as well as "Soon" and "I Got a Crush on You," a characteristic adaptation of a current slang phrase and oblique declaration of affection.

The Gershwins closed the year of the successful *Strike Up the Band*—1930—with a return to the fatuous Twenties-like libretto of *Girl Crazy,* despite which they created one of their richest scores. The book may have been forgettable, but the songs remain: "I Got Rhythm," "Embraceable You," "But Not for Me," and more. The sound and the language of this score left the Jazz Age behind.

This was further demonstrated by *Of Thee I Sing* (1931), the first musical to be awarded a Pulitzer Prize. Like their earlier political operetta, this satire was thoroughly integrated, though its title song, as well as "Wintergreen for President," "Who Cares?" and "Love is Sweeping the Country," did well on their own. *Sing's* sequel, *Let "Em Eat Cake* (1933), one of the Gershwin's most significant scores, failed miserably. Ira believed that this was so because its book was down on everything (including the government); George felt it had failed because it had no love story (but it did have their wonderful, contrapuntal "Mine").

All during the prolific years working on Broadway with Ira, George was branching out into the "serious" world of classical music. Most American critics were not in Gershwin's corner when his symphonic music debuted; he was taken seriously in Europe long before musicologists and critics rediscovered him at home. During his lifetime critics kept hoping he would turn out to be an American Bach, Beethoven, or some other imported luminary. Instead, he turned out to be the American Gershwin. Once *Rhapsody in Blue* (1924) established him in the concert world, it was followed by the more traditional *Concerto in F* (1925) and the exceptionally orchestrated *An American in Paris* (1928). Since their inception, these compositions have been played and recorded all over the world. Although not instant hits as were the big three, the *Second Rhapsody, Cuban Overture,* and *Variations on "I Got Rhythm"* would eventually come into their own in concert performances and recordings.

Each of these works, in its own genre, was a harbinger. In his first rhapsody, George set out, and succeeded, in composing with an American accent. This disturbed many critics, who preferred their serious music, no matter who wrote it, with a German, or if one were really "modern," French accent. The critics, too, had a problem with his Tin Pan Alley roots and found it perturbing that a mere songwriter could write rhapsodies, concertos, preludes, and heavens to Betsy, an opera. Another factor bothered them: his popularity.

But it was as if the general music-loving public didn't read the pundits. If the wide popularity of his songs was disturbing, the popularity of the concert works, especially the big three—*Rhapsody in Blue, Concerto in F;* and *An American in Paris*—rendered critics superfluous. This is not to suggest that Gershwin did not have his champions among the critics. He did. In addition, some of his greatest "fans" were men of musical grandeur: composer-pianist Sergi Rachmaninoff, composers Maurice Ravel and Bela Bartok, violinist Jascha Heifetz, and many others.

Not all of George's more serious work, however, was immediately appreciated by audiences. The now classic *Porgy and Bess* was a commercial failure when introduced by the Theatre Guild in 1935. But the American-inflected richness of the score and the humanity of the play have made it, over the years, a prodigiously loved work. *Porgy and Bess* has found its place in the repertoire of the New York Metropolitan Opera, La Scala, and other world-class companies, and has even been cheered by audiences throughout the Eastern Bloc.

But after *Porgy's* initial "failure," the Gershwins turned toward Hollywood, then at the peak of the Astaire and Rogers film-musical renaissance. Alas, the front-office types feared that George had gone "highbrow." George denied it, saying that he was "out to write hits"—an assertion he proved once he and Ira had settled into Beverly Hills in the summer of 1936.

There they created the evergreens for *Shall We Dance*—"They Can't Take That Away From Me" and "Slap That Bass"—and for *A Damsel in Distress*—"A Foggy Day," "Nice Work If You Can Get It." They were working on *The Goldwyn Follies* when George began to manifest the symptoms of what was revealed to be a brain tumor. Surgery proved unsuccessful, and George Gershwin died, aged 38, on July 11, 1937.

The death of his brother did not end Ira Gershwin's career. After some time off, he began working on songs with Jerome Kern and Harry Warren. Then came a major Broadway offer resulting in a remarkable success, *Lady in the Dark* (1941), with music by Kurt Weill. Ira proceeded to work with Weill on a couple of film scores and a beautifully scored flop, *The Firebrand of Florence*.

He did even better in Hollywood, whose relative serenity he treasured. With Harry Warren he did the score that reunited Astaire and Rogers, *The Barkleys of Broadway* (1949); with Burton Lane he collaborated on good songs for a bad movie, *Give a Girl a Break* (1953). The next year he worked with Harold Arlen on the Judy Garland classic, *A Star is Born* (1954), with its unforgettable "The Man That Got Away."

He took time out to write his book *Lyrics on Several Occasions* (1959), and then quietly retired to prepare and annotate the papers of the brothers Gershwin for preservation in the Library of Congress. Ira's peaceful death on August 17, 1983, closed an extraordinary era in the history of American music and song, one that endowed us with a rich—and unmistakably Gershwinesque—legacy.

Scott Joplin Rags, Genius Brought No Riches — Just a New Art Form

Mike Flanagan

Scott Joplin (Courtesy of the Institute of Jazz Studies, Rutgers University).

Scott Joplin's effect on American music cannot be underestimated. In a time before the music business was radio, stereo, or compact disc, he composed a body of work that elevated popular music to an art form.

The ragtime Mozart was a Westerner, born in Texas thirty-two years after the fall of the Alamo and nurtured in the home state of Jesse James. His accomplishments are all the more remarkable when we consider his bumpy personal life and the bigoted times in which he lived.

Joplin was born Nov. 24, 1868, on the Texas side of the town that would become Texarkana, where his father was working as a railroad laborer. He was the second of six children.

Giles Joplin, his father, was a former slave from North Carolina who had obtained legal freedom around 1863. His Kentucky mother, Florence Givens Joplin, was born free. The family was far from rich: Florence cursed the bags of laundry she took in. But they loved music.

Giles was an accomplished "plantation violinist," having played everything from waltzes to polkas in the finest mansions. Florence sang in the Sunday choir and played the banjo. She could see that Scott was the most musically adept of the family band, jamming away on a hollow guitar.

When a neighbor heard him play her piano, she gave him open access to the instrument. For his seventh birthday (and Christmas and the next birthday, insisted Giles), Scott was given a used piano, on which he spent all his free time.

By eleven, Joplin had caught the attention of an elderly German music teacher. In three years of study with him, Joplin received a classical background, learned to read music, improved his technique, and began composing.

His training was cut short at age fourteen, when his mother died. Joplin left home soon after, possibly because his father thought he was spending too much time on his music.

His teens were spent playing in bars, brothels, cafes, steamboats, wherever the tinkling of a piano was required atmosphere. From Texas to Nebraska and back, he provided the sound track in a variety of houses, from Scar Face Mary's in Oklahoma City to Chicago's plush Everleigh Club.

The kind of music he played was an early version of ragtime, an evolving joyful noise with roots in Africa. Music had come over on the slave galleys, but white owners often forbade the folk sounds. By blending the African rhythms with European musical discipline and counterpoint, the syncopated melodies were made "acceptable."

Original American music developed. Plantation reviews begat minstrel shows, which introduced the country to new dance music that included the two-step and the cakewalk.

In 1893, Joplin and other itinerant "ticklers" congregated at the Chicago World's Columbian Exposition. Heartened by the crowd response, he moved to Sedalia, Mo, to compose. Musical horizons expanded further at the George R. Smith College for Negroes. He played and arranged for the Queen City Concert Band and the Texas Medley Quartet.

Joplin had penned his first rags by 1897, but publishers were reluctant to accept them. After rejection in Sedalia, his first sale of the new music was "Original Rags" to the Carl Hoffman house in Kansas City. Reflecting the predominant ugly racial atmosphere of the day, the sheet music cover depicted an old black rag picker in front of a dilapidated shack.

At Sedalia's Maple Leaf Club, the new sounds rocked the rafters. Here, Joplin met music publisher John Stark, forming the team that would change musical history. In September 1899, Stark published Joplin's "Maple Leaf Rag." Sales were phenomenal; fifty thousand copies sold in the first few months.

The song brought Joplin international attention as it became the first sheet music in history to sell more than a million copies. He and Stark, sharing royalties, moved to St. Louis, setting up a hit factory that produced "The Entertainer," "Peacherine Rag," and "Fig Leaf Rag." Later that year, he staged an ambitious ballet, "The Ragtime Dance," in Sedalia.

Ragtime became an immensely popular, forbidden rage. Because of its bawdy origins, "respectability" was a major issue in turn-of-the-century America, one that never really resolved itself. The racist climate of the day figured heavily in the uproar, as white and black music styles intertwined. "The country is awakening to the real harm these 'coon songs' and 'ragtime' are doing," spouted one editorial. An official statement from the American Federation of Musicians, meeting in Denver in 1901, called ragtime "musical rot."

Despite the controversy, his music was in demand. Joplin became obsessed with giving ragtime a place of honor. Thanks to modern technology, he could be heard across the country. The Pianola (player piano) offered a crude playback system from piano rolls. Joplin recorded many of his famous pieces in New York. By putting the paper roll inside the piano cabinet and pushing the foot pedals, one could hear Scott Joplin's ragtime in the parlor.

Joplin's personal life was not nearly as bright. At thirty-one, he had achieved enough financial success to wed Belle Hayden, the sister-in-law of one of his music pupils; but the marriage was one of turmoil and problems. Belle had little understanding of her husband's genius—as their funds dropped while he composed the ragtime opera "A Guest of Honor," so did her patience.

A child died in infancy in 1903. Their marriage fell apart soon after, and Belle died suddenly in 1905. Haunted but still driven, Scott Joplin again became a nomadic "professor."

Always the womanizer, Joplin's torrid romances now found their way into compositions such as "The Antoinette March," and "Leola." One of his most brilliant rags was "The Cascades," a rolling, flowing piece inspired by the Cascades Gardens at the 1904 St. Louis World's Fair.

In 1907 he moved to New York, married Lottie Stokes, and stabilized for a while. Lottie ran a rooming house for performers, allowing her husband freedom and the time to compose works such as "Rose Leaf" and "Sugar Cane." He also penned "The School of Ragtime," six exercises for the serious student. But his consuming passion was the creation of an Afro-American folk opera, "Treemonisha."

The last ten years of his life were spent on the project, a moralistic tale of what education could do for the black race. In 1911, he paid to have the 270-page vocal/piano score published.

Popular music tastes were again changing, something Joplin had failed to notice in his operatic trance. Attempts to find a producer for the show failed. In 1915, Joplin gave a solo performance of the work in Harlem to an invited audience.

Depression from the failure of "Treemonisha" along with an advancing case of syphilis contracted during his early years on the road slowly unraveled his sanity. By 1916, his condition had so deteriorated that Lottie was forced to commit him to the Manhattan State Hospital on Ward's Island.

Cause of death, April 1, 1917, was listed as "dementia paralytica." He was forty-nine. "You know," said Lottie, "he would often say that he'd never be appreciated until after he was dead."

Director George Hill heard a Joplin recording by Joshua Rifkin while working on his 1973 film, "The Sting."

The motion picture, starring Paul Newman and Robert Redford, took place in the Chicago of the Twenties, but Hill thought the Joplin humor and style would make the perfect sound track. "The Entertainer" became "The Sting's" theme song.

In addition to the film's winning the best-picture Oscar the following year, the theme and score won Academy Awards.

By the end of 1974, the Scott Joplin sound track had sold more than two million copies and a full-scale revival was under way. In Sedalia, they held the Scott Joplin Ragtime Festival. "Treemonisha" enjoyed a Broadway revival in 1975. Its composer was awarded a posthumous Pulitzer Price in 1975.

For years, Joplin had shared an unmarked pauper's grave with two others at St. Michael's Cemetery in Astoria, Queens. The "rediscovery" earned him a bronze marker. During the ceremonies conducted by the American Society of Composers, Authors and Publishers, a gentle breeze blew maple leaves over the grave. Historical vindication had come for "The King of the Ragtime Composers." His genius had come full circle.

Thelonious Monk: 1917–1982
The Man Who Altered the Language of Jazz

Robert Palmer

Thelonious Monk (Courtesy of the Institute of Jazz Studies, Rutgers University).

Thelonious Sphere Monk, the pianist and composer who died February 17, 1982 in Englewood Hospital in New Jersey after suffering a stroke, made music that defied time and seemed to defy gravity. His music was a challenge with which each generation of modern jazz musicians has had to grapple: he played a particularly crucial role in the maturation of Bud Powell, John Coltrane and Cecil Taylor, among others. And many rock musicians have long been ardent Monk fans, including NRBQ's Terry Adams (who once assembled an album of unissued Monk performances for Columbia Records) and the J. Geils band.

Though Monk—who was born in Rocky Mount, North Carolina, on October 10th, 1917, and moved to Manhattan with his mother at age four—presided over the birth of bebop in the Forties, he himself was no bebopper. He gained experience playing behind a healing preacher when he was in his teens, and the influence of the Harlem stride style exemplified by Fats Waller and James P. Johnson often cropped up in his playing. Neither was Monk a traditionalist. The compositions he began writing in the Forties moved in herky-jerky lurches and heaving wave rhythms: their melodies and harmonies were as jagged as shards of exploded gun metal.

Though his classic and comparatively gentle "Round Midnight" was recorded by Cootie Williams in 1944, it wasn't until 1947, when Monk began making records for the fledgling Blue Note label, that the world at large began to hear what he was up to. And what on earth *was* he up to? "Thelonious," a tune from his very first Blue Note session, had verses fashioned from a single ingeniously hammered note, with three horns playing shifting dissonances behind it. He developed the one-note motif in his solo and then abruptly broke into some pure, old-fashioned Harlem oompah stride.

Monk's work was too abstract for most musicians, let alone the general public, and he performed sporadically. Then, in 1951, he was busted when a friend's car, in which he was sitting, was searched and found to contain narcotics. According to every musician's and critic's view of the incident, the dope belonged to Monk's friend. But Monk refused to tell the cops, which cost him sixty days in jail—and six years of work, because of a New York law that forbade anyone with a criminal record from working in nightclubs.

So Monk simply stayed in his apartment on Manhattan's West Sixty-third Street, venturing out occasionally to make some brilliant recordings for Prestige. He had never been much of a bon vivant anyway; his family, a very few close friends and the ordinary folks on his block were the only people he ever seemed to socialize with. *New York Times* jazz critic John S. Wilson remembers witnessing an hour-long "conversation" between Monk and Duke Ellington—Monk's part consisted entirely of barely audible grunts. But he could be outgoing. At New York's Village Vanguard one night, he began dancing (a favorite pastime) with the young son of a musician friend and became so exuberant he overturned a table.

When Monk returned to the clubs in 1957, he put together a quartet, with John Coltrane on tenor sax, for his debut at the Five Spot. The experience stamped Coltrane indelibly with Monk's rigorously logical, utterly original slant on rhythm and harmony. In a sense, though, it still wasn't Monk's time. A few exceptional pianists played his tunes and incorporated traces of his pungency—Bud Powell, of course, and Randy Watson and Elmo Hope. But while the most adept hornmen could navigate the treacherous rapids of his compositions when he was at the keyboard, jabbing and prodding them on, his skewed angles and diamond-hard minimalism still hadn't worked their way into the mainstream of jazz language. Miles Davis and John Coltrane recorded a lovely and popular rendition of "Round Midnight" in 1955, and a few adventuresome souls were playing a handful of his less "difficult" tunes—"Epistrophy," "Straight, No Chaser," "Bemsha Swing" and the heartfelt ballad "Ruby, My Dear." But nobody, absolutely nobody, cared to tackle, say, "Nutty" (a pummeling line that sounds like an early template for Coltrane's playing in his last years), or the diabolical, logically illogical "Played Twice."

Finally, in the early Sixties, a few major musicians, such as Eric Dolphy and Cecil Taylor, developed personal languages that incorporated some of Monk's angularity and the watch-me-now excitement of his rhythmic juggling acts. Steve Lacy, a soprano saxophonist who played in a couple of Monk's bands, put together an early-Sixties quartet that played nothing but Monk, and beginning in 1959, Monk had a regular band, with the dependable and frequently ingenious Charlie Rouse on tenor saxophone.

Monk's health began to fail him in the early Seventies, and he played less frequently. His last concert appearance was at Carnegie Hall in 1976. During his last years, he and his wife, Nellie, reportedly lived on the New Jersey estate of the Baroness Pannonica ("Nica") de Koenigwharter, the longtime patroness of major jazz musicians, in whose New York apartment Charlie Parker died. In 1981, some of the foremost interpreters of Monk's music—Rouse, Lacy, the pianists Barry Harris, Muhal Richard Abrams and Anthony Davis, plus others—presented two concerts with an all-Monk repertoire. And now that jazz seems to be entering a period of classicism, with some of the most adventurous musicians also devoting themselves to reinterpreting the tradition, Monk's time may have come at last. If so, at least his wife of many years and his children, Thelonious Jr. and Barbara (members of the funk band T.S. Monk), are here to appreciate it.

It's difficult to say whether Monk was simply far ahead of his time or somehow operated outside time altogether. "He wrote the way he thought, and he presented it to people whether they liked it or not," said Charlie Rouse, who played with Monk for eleven years—longer than any other musician. "I doubt that people are going to realize until years from now how great a contribution he made to America."

Chapter 3
The Big Bands

Where have the big bands gone? This is a question often asked in conversations about the swing era. This was an era that found people in our society listening (theaters) or dining and dancing (hotels) or dancing at ballrooms across the country. The big bands were everywhere. Some we relegated to specific geographic territories where they had developed a faithful clientele. Others toured from coast-to-coast playing all types of communities from theaters to ballrooms (also known as dance halls). Recordings of the big bands enjoyed tremendous sales until the ban was instituted by the head of the Musicians' Union. The ban forbade instrumentalists from recording. This decision was a major contributor to the demise of the bands. The popularity of the era never recovered.

Mike Vax, former trumpeter and road manager with the Stan Kenton band, stated his view on what happened. Vax, following his years with Kenton, formed his own band in an effort to help revive the era. Unfortunately, it was an economic impossibility. Today, he performs regularly with his small group and is in demand nationwide as a soloist and clinician. He has appeared with the author's university band at a successful jazz festival. An excellent performer, he enjoys working with young musicians in an effort to give jazz proper direction.

Mike Vax solos with the Stan Kenton Band (Courtesy: Mike Vax Collection).

What Happened to the Big Bands?

Mike Vax Poses the Question

One of the questions that is most asked at my clinic is: "Whatever happened to the big band era?" This question is a universal one among that dedicated, enthusiastic, almost fanatic group of people called "Big Band Fans." The age variation of this small but vocal breed is like no other in the world. There is no age barrier for those who love the big band. I have seen nine and ten-year-olds in grammar school who are completely captivated at their first experience with a big band. I have also known people in their eighties who have loved the sound for over fifty years. It seems that the combination of brass, saxes, and rhythm playing music that has a beat has always been able to stir the soul of certain people all over the world.

Why, then, are there only a few bands left? Why is it so hard for anyone to get a new big band started? These are very important questions to me, because, as many of you know, I tried starting a big band of my own!

17

I think that we should start the discussion of these questions at the beginning. The first big bands were, of course, strictly dance bands. They almost always worked in hotels such as the St. Francis and the Fairmont in San Francisco. These hotels had dance bands performing in them as early as 1913. Other important cities for the early dance bands were Chicago, Los Angeles, and New York. Some of the early leaders were Art Hickman, Jan Garber, Paul Whiteman, Meyer Davis and Ted Lewis, just to name a few. Many of these bands started out with quite a different type of instrumentation from what we are familiar with today. A typical band might have had trumpet, clarinet, violin, piano, drums, and a couple of banjos. If you have ever heard an old 78 record of a very early dance band, you know just how different they sounded.

Big bands were a very dominant force in popular music in the twenties, thirties, and forties. This was really the "big band era." These were the big name bands that toured all over the U.S., and literally hundreds of "territory" and hotel bands. The territory bands traveled mainly in the Midwest area. They played a circuit of ballrooms over a three or four-state area. The hotel bands found a "home" at a certain hotel and stayed in that spot for a long period of time. Some bands stayed for many years at the same hotel.

During the big band era, people made a practice of going out to ballrooms and hotels to hear and dance to the famous bands. (Remember that there was no television, and few people could afford a large record collection.) It became a very big event when a traveling band came to town. Literally thousands of people would turn out at the local ballroom.

All the well-known musicians and singers came out of the ranks of these big bands. Popular music revolved around such people as Benny Goodman, the Dorseys, the Casa Loma Orchestra, Duke Ellington, Jimmy Lunceford, Buddy Rogers, Harry James, Glenn Miller, and many, many others.

In the late thirties and early forties, bands started getting away from playing only dance music and got more into jazz for listening. Many leaders experimented with getting new sounds out of their orchestras. A big influence on this type of big band sound was my old boss, Stan Kenton. He has been an innovator ever since the early days at Balboa Ballroom. After the Second World War, the decline of the big bands started. Popular music was changing, and many singers became more famous than the bands they had started with. In the late forties, television started to become popular and people were staying home at night instead of going out to the ballrooms. High-fidelity long-playing records also became popular in the fifties. People could listen to their favorite band in their own home. With all of these things pulling the public away from the ballrooms and theaters, the demise of the big band era was imminent. The expense of keeping a band on the road also became a factor. It became more expensive every year.

The music business took a huge downward plunge in the fifties. Singers and groups became popular that were mediocre at best. Music itself became little more than three-chord trash, and "payola" became the normal way of getting radio air play. Electronics in a studio could make a few musicians sound like a whole orchestra. The big band and orchestra were just not needed in the hurry of the recording companies to make a fast buck. These companies did not care at all about the quality of the records they churned out, as long as they sold a lot of copies in a short period of time.

During the sixties, things took a turn for the better. Popular music started becoming more meaningful, and the musicians were of a much higher caliber than those of the fifties. It was with the turn of the decade from the fifties to the sixties that the jazz education movement really took hold.

With this movement came a resurgence of interest in the big bands. The students involved in this movement were more interested in listening to the big bands than in dancing to them.

Along with this listening movement came a renewed interest by the "older generation" for the nostalgia of dancing to the old big bands. These two separate factors helped bring a new vitality to the bands that already had big names. This interest is growing in strength even today. Bands such as Stan Kenton, Woody Herman, Buddy Rich, Maynard Ferguson, Harry James, and Count Basie are enjoying great success. Also, the bands of the Duke Ellington, Tommy and Jimmy Dorsey, and Glenn Miller organizations are doing very well under new leaders.

With this revitalization of interest in the big bands, we might be inclined to think that the beginning of a new big band era is at hand. As much as I love the big band sound, I am afraid that there is no possibility of a new age of fifteen to twenty-piece bands traveling all over the country. There are many reasons for this pessimistic outlook. The first and foremost reason is economic. It is just too expensive to put together a full-time band to travel by bus or car, playing one-nighters. Fuel, hotel, and food costs have all risen a hundred per cent or more in the past ten years. A new big band with no real name would have to lose money for years before it could hope to return the slightest profit. Even the established name bands don't make a big profit from their road tours today. They rely on record sales and publishing profits to help support the band.

There have been many well-known musicians, such as Clark Terry, Louis Bellson, Ed Shaughnessy, Bill Berry, Dee Barton, Les Hooper, John Von Ohlen, Bill Watrous, and Lin Biviano, who have tried to get big bands off the ground in recent years. Some of these crusaders have met with modest success, but none have achieved enough support to really get out on the road and make an extended tour.

The only two new big bands that really have "made it" in the last ten years are Thad Jones-Mel Lewis and Don Ellis. One important fact to remember, though, is that neither band has stayed on the road for an extended period of time. Both bands have made tours and then gone back home, because many of the musicians in these bands are studio players who can't afford to be away too long.

Don Ellis' band has had a long period of inactivity because Don has been ill, but the band is back together now and Glen Stuart (the lead trumpet player) runs the band for Don. The Thad Jones-Mel Lewis band still plays every Monday night at the Village Vanguard in New York. They make short tours every once in a while and still put out very interesting and exciting records. This band is the personification of the big band of the future: a part-time band that plays in a club once or twice a week and makes short tours. Its members will have studio or other "in-town" jobs, and perform with the big band for an artistic treat. The band would have to find some record company that is interested in *quality* rather than *quantity,* to put out its records. This is easier said than done, because record companies are *notorious* for not caring about artistic endeavor. Let us hope, as with the Bill Watrous Band (which has two fantastic records out), some of the companies will see the light.

One way of making meaningful records is to put out your own. Many people, such as Stan Kenton, George Shearing, The Four Freshmen, Clark Terry, and myself have all followed this route. The sales aren't as high as with a major company, but at least interest can be created.

There is one other possibility to help keep the big band movement alive. For want of a better name, I will call it the little-big band. I think that Maynard Ferguson has the right idea with his band. The traveling band of the future will have to contain no more ten to fourteen musicians. This hypothetical band will play a fusion of jazz and rock elements. It will continue the tradition and sound of the big bands, but with

Maynard Ferguson

fewer members. It will perform a good percentage of its jobs at the high schools, colleges, and universities that have jazz education programs. It will do clinics in the afternoon for the music students, and then perform a concert that night. It will have a dance book, but dances will not be a big part of its performing schedule.

It will, as with the automobile of the future, be smaller and more economical, but just as exciting as its larger predecessors.

Let us hope that these projections (or *wishes* of a big band fanatic, if you like) will come true. Most of the leaders of today's big name bands are in their fifties or older. We need new blood in the big band business. It would be a shame if, ten years from now, there were only "ghost bands".

I challenge any musician who is reading this article:

If you really care about the big band as a musical entity, then form rehearsal bands and experiment with new instrumentations and sounds. Don't be discouraged by setbacks or lack of interest. Keep the faith! Somewhere out there are the big band leaders of the future!

Dr. Herb Wong, one of the leading exponents on big band jazz, is also an independent record producer. Under the label of *Palo Alto Jazz Records,* Wong assembled musicians for record dates and produced recordings for the general public. This is a difficult task, considering the market for pure jazz compared to the various forms and artists of rock. In addition Wong is one of the most popular adjudicators at competitive jazz festivals. Past president of the National Association of Jazz Educators, Wong has been a driving force in the promotion of big bands in schools, one of the last frontiers of the big band jazz. A close friend and associate of the late Woody Herman, Wong has written a tribute to the jazz man, indicating Herman's willingness to help young musicians. The following article was written prior to the bandleader's passing.

Thundering from the Campuses:
Woody Herman's Herds and Jazz Education

Dr. Herbert Wong

Woody Herman's "Herds" have been extraordinary mobile jazz laboratories—universities on the road for young jazz players since the early days. However, in synch with the proliferation of jazz education programs, Woody's bands have been hospitable, coveted destinations/habitats for college-university and conservatory-trained musicians, especially in the last 25 years.

A true living legend, Woody has reached his 50th year as a jazz band leader and he occupies this amazing historical seat while he continues to blaze the road throughout most of the calendar year with his "Young Thundering Herd"—a joyful, relentlessly swinging band. Les Brown and Lionel Hampton are two other swing era band leaders who intermittently front their own groups—Hamp much more regularly than Brown. With the passing of Ellington, Basie, James, Kenton and Goodman—just a small handful of big bands still play the composite of contemporary venues such as festivals, theaters, hotels, country clubs, music camps, amusement parks, jazz clubs, shopping malls, casinos and loads of school/college campuses. Buddy Rich, Maynard Ferguson, Toshiko Akiyoshi and a few others along with Woody Herman fill the bulk of these pipelines.

The unique dynamics of the Herman band environment finds musicians gaining sustained musical/psychological support from Woody, reflecting his values on the growth and development of each musician in his band. Simply ask any of the many hundreds of graduates of "The Herds" and you'll get a confirmation of Woody's philosophy/system, told perhaps in numerous different ways but landing in convergent territory. In essence, they dig working with him and not just for him—the feelings couched in mutual respect and gratitude.

"Woody extracted the best of me, toward my personal and musical growth. I also learned how to be a sustaining musician on the road, preparing me for my professional future. It was an irreplaceable experience!" These are sentiments of pianist Andy LaVerne who was with Woody in the 70's before joining Stan Getz' band. I have interviewed scores of Woody's band members through the years and LaVerne's recent comments typify the general feedback. Trombonist Phil Wilson, a faculty member of the Berklee College of Music, made vital contributions to the 1962–65 Herds when his distinctive bone solos helped to characterize the sounds and energetic spirit of that great band. He told me several years ago another positive, common remembrance: "Woody had a way of cutting out the fat and getting right to the meat of an arrangement and to the audience." And his personality was the same—he allowed the guys to relax and be them-

Woody Herman (Courtesy: Ingrid Herman Reese Collection).

selves musically and personally . . . until it got out of whack. Then ''The Chopper'' would come in and take care of business. He looked at everything that way—tolerant although not patient! Woody's band was the idol band—everyone wanted to be on it. About twelve of us who were at Berklee as students got on the band through our experience with Herb Pomeroy's band at Berklee and the NORAD ''Commanders'' Band (The North American Air Defense Command Orchestra). Bill Chase, Gordon Brisker, Jake Hanna, Chuck Andres, Paul Fontaine, Larry Cavalli, Jerry Lamy and Bob Rudolph were all hungry and wanted to be in the best big band in the land, and our dreams were answered with Woody.''

Turning the clock back to the bands of the late forties and the fifties, the majority of the alumni of Kenton and Herman bands got off the road and dominated the lucrative-based L.A. studios. Outstanding players

Woody Herman and Herb Wong (Courtesy: Herb Wong Collection).

in this migration included the likes of Joe Mondragon, Shelly Manne, Shorty Rogers, Bud Shank, Milt Bernhardt, the Condoli Brothers, Bob Cooper, Conrad Gozzo, Al Porcina, Larry Bunker and Jack Nimitz among many more in the New York, Chicago and Las Vegas circuits in addition to L.A. Yet others chose to become involved with leading their own groups: e.g., Stan Getz, Zoot Sims, Al Cohn, Urbie Green, Terry Gibbs and Gene Ammons.

By the late fifties and early sixties, this existing process depleted the rosters significantly, creating gaping spaces for replacements to fill. Overlapping perhaps in a providential way or at least via a vigorous twist of fate, a number of early maturing jazz education curricula/programs had coincidentally developed a ripe crop of young, well-schooled university students who began to filter into key roles of the Herman, Kenton and Rich big bands. These bright graduates were recruited from the highly reputed, powerful pioneer

The Woody Herman Thundering Herd (Courtesy: Ingrid Herman Reese Collection).

programs of North Texas State University and Berklee College in the main—percursors to the profluence of many dozens of sophisticated jazz studies departments and hundreds of jazz ensembles with a layered network of high school feeder programs.

In retrospect, the replacements comprised of many gifted performers and writers from rich campus resources, from many parts of the country, renewed a critical supply line of eager, fiery young talent, meeting the demands of the professional orchestras which virtually became the few true "post-grad" citadels in the idiom. In the opinion of most aspirants and alumni of Woody's band, his was a well-matched symbiotic relationship with the musicians.

In a recent discussion I had with Woody in September following his performance at a jazz festival in Palo Alto, California, he waxed enthusiastically over the state of the art linking his band specifically with jazz education over the years. In response to my query regarding his assessment of jazz education from his

Charlotte and Woody Herman (Courtesy: Ingrid Herman Reese Collection).

perspective, Woody said: "I'm asked very frequently around the world about how and where does the band get such talented musicians. I think there's no doubt about the successful job that's being done and we in the U.S.A. are an object of admiration, and even some healthy envy.

"These young men come to the band with impressive chops, with well grounded musical theory and knowledge of the history of the music and can handle any style of playing. It wasn't always like this, you know. Over all, very seldom does any of them miss the reasons or meaning for our music . . . and I mean the future of the music. As for your question about their capabilities as I have seen them, I'm really blown away by the way they can, on one take, sight read the most complex charts, out in front of them for the first time. In the past, this high level of ability was not easy to find. Of course, there are more ways and people to help the young students than any past point in history—all sorts of wonderful books, charts, improv workshop techniques, records, tapes, videos, on and on. What a different scene it is today!"

Woody is known for his generous approach of providing extended time and space for each newcomer on the band, permitting him leeway to interpret the band's music in his own way. Former drummer with Woody—Ed Soph, a product of NTSU who has served the band on a number of segments, confirms Woody's tactic. Ed describes, "Woody will give you complete freedom to interpret the music, and since you're on his band, he feels you're musically mature for him to give you that freedom, and if you blow it, he'll say something. But he often doesn't say much, but when he does, it's always right on the button—right there, and it's like the clouds part and it's all clear. This applies to arrangements as well. A good example is when Frank Tiberi's chart for Coltrane's "Countdown" was rehearsed. Woody just sat there checking it out. After the first time it was played, he said nothing. We played it again. And he said, "Frank, the shout chorus doesn't fit with the rest of the chart. It needs to be more syncopated like the sax solo." Woody hit it right on the head. Frank re-wrote that chorus and everything locked in perfectly! And there are dozens of other examples."

Frank Tiberi independently commented about the same incident. "Everyone who writes for the band as a band member grows with Woody. For instance, on "Countdown," he told me that the last part was great but it needed to be flashed up and, of course, now it's really exciting! Alan Broadbent and Gary Anderson who have written fine charts became really good writers, helped by Woody's keen ears and sense of editing. I think Woody is a patient man . . . he edits and corrects while he allows them to stay on the band to mature. I've been with the band about 18 years and I've seen him hold these values for a lot of guys. Nothing goes by

Martha Raye and Woody Herman (Courtesy: Ingrid Herman Reese Collection).

him without him noticing it, but he seldom shows this in any demonstrable way. But he is incredibly on target. He helps to get people relaxed so they can get quality musicianship and quality presentation of a tune.''

Woody has strong views about how jazz studies programs can help young players in their improvised solo work. ''I firmly believe things would be much more improved if *guidance* were given to the players about alternative ideas and approaches. A wide variety of different ways to compensate what might turn out to be a narrow perspective for the players is a need, I think, that could be filled *before* they leave the campus searching for a professional endeavor.''

''Of course, today we have professional jazz clinicians who are, in many cases, products of the jazz education movement, and they are familiar with what's needed out in the real music world and what would be effective in clinical situations. They are able to provide students and instructors with high quality guidance.'' Campus clinics are common educational fare for the Herman bands as they have presented practicums nearly every week for over 20 years, along with their concerts. Some of the finest pro clinicians incubated in the Herds—e.g., Ed Soph, Steve Houghton, Bobby Shew, Phil Wilson, Roger Pemberton and Willie Thomas come to mind.

Regarding the severe lack of professional playing opportunities for the disproportionately large number of excellent young jazz players, Woody recommended unhesitatingly, ''I think these interested young men and women should be schooled in some solid alternative field such as computer science, get a steady day gig in the field, and then practice every night after work for a few years. Get a playing gig in town until the time and opportunity for the music is more receptive. Of course, there are always exceptions to the norm, in which case worthy players by some circumstantial quirk will find a viable niche in music within a reasonably short time.''

Returning to some thoughts about young arrangers—composers in the last dozen years or so, I mentioned pianists John Oddo and Alan Broadbent, trumpeters Tony Klatka and Bill Stapleton, saxophonist Gary Anderson and trombonist John Fedchock to Woody. He asserted, ''Most of the budding writers arrive like rough diamonds. Gary Anderson, for instance, who has become a highly successful writer for a variety of media, started meagerly but matured dramatically. He worked very hard at it. I had asked him to arrange Aaron Copland's ''Fanfare for the Common Man'' after I heard the guys fooling around with its opening theme. It's become one of the most important staples in our book in the last decade. All of the writers you mentioned understood what the band needed simply because they were integrally involved with our music.

25

L to R: Louis Armstrong, Woody Herman and Phil Wilson (Courtesy: Herb Wong Collection).

John Oddo and, of course, John Fedchock, are the most recent major contributors and both are very special talents who have their undefinable spark.'' Speaking of Fedchock, who is a graduate of The Ohio State U. and its great jazz ensemble, and holds a Masters of Jazz from Eastman, he was inspired when he was in high school in Highland Heights, Ohio. ''Of all the big bands, Woody's has always been my favorite. Ever since Woody came to play at my school in 1974, I had wanted to play in his band. As a matter of fact, that concert was one of the things that inspired me to go into music,'' reflects John. ''In this day and age, without being on a band like this one, there would be very little opportunity for me to do the two things I love most—writing and playing jazz.''

Woody Herman, a dynamic force in jazz and jazz education, creates a gang of thunder from the campuses, and in turn he coaches them to swing to the high heavens. We all dig you, Woody! Happy giant 50th!

From his beginnings in jazz at Ithaca Conservatory to Duke University, to New York and the professional world of dance bands, Les Brown has carved an undisputable niche in the development of the big bands. His band is one of the very, very few big bands still playing today. The Les Brown Band has earned the reputation as being one of the very finest of the big bands. He considers himself the leader of a ''dance band,'' since this was the original concept of the big bands. A shrewd business man, Brown has kept his band together through turbulent years of economic setbacks, interest in other forms of music (such as rock), and diminishing activity in the recording industry in relation to big bands. His band is under the effective managership of his brother, trombonist, ''Stumpy'' Brown who handles the bands logistics, personnel, travel arrangements, and bookings.

In the following interview, Les Brown describes his personal career as well as the development and demise of the big bands. A very personable individual, he enjoys performing and has no plans for retirement.

Les Brown Interview

February 13, 1988, Pacific Palisades, California

Q: When did you realize you wanted to become a band leader?

Les: I can't give you an exact answer to that, what year or anything, but it seemed like I had a band in high school, and another when I went to Ithaca conservatory. I had a band when I was in military school, and a band at Duke University. I came out of Duke University with a band, and I've been going ever since, so I guess I must have been kind of young.

Q: When you started, did you have any specific heroes that motivated you to say, "Hey, I want to be like him!"?

Les: Well, I admired certain bands that were extant at the time—Paul Whiteman, for one, Isham Jones, and then a little later the Casa Loma Band. I enjoyed them. Of course, I was also doing legitimate work. I played as a saxophone soloist in 1928 with Conway's band down at Wildwood, New Jersey. I don't know if anybody remembers Pat Conway, but he was sort of second to Sousa in the concert band field. Then, of course, when Benny Goodman, Tommy Dorsey and those came along, I changed my style a little with my Duke University Band.

Q: When you first organized your professional band, were there any special processes or procedures you used, such as getting an arranger, getting a book, getting an agent, things of that nature?

Les: Well, we came out of Duke University pretty well-organized. The band had been together under my leadership for two years. We had nothing but special arrangements. We didn't use stocks in those days, and that gave us more or less of a style. And so we were pretty well-organized when we came out, and luckily we had a job up in New Jersey at Bud Lake. People from Decca Records found us, heard the band, and signed us to a record contract. We've been going ever since.

Q: Were you the leader of the Duke Blue Devils when you were at the University?

Les: Yes, I was the leader all four years I was there, but my name wasn't in front of the band until my junior year. The gentlemen who had the band encouraged me, in fact twisted my arm and got me down to Duke instead of the University of Pennsylvania. I had to rehearse the band, make arrangements and everything all the time I was at Duke, so I guess I became a leader my freshman year.

Q: In the music business, what percentage of being a band leader is being a musician, a businessman, a psychologist, a booking agent, and whatever else that has to be done?

Les: I couldn't give you an exact percentage, but you have to be a little of each. Psychologist, so you can get along with the fellows in the band and know how to treat them. It always helps to be a musician, although some of our most successful leaders don't know a note of music, but it helps. Businessman—I always had somebody to help me in that. I'm not the greatest businessman in the world, but I always had a good booking agent, especially when I got Joe Glaser, who was my "angel". He bankrolled the band for the first four or five years 'til we finally started making some money, and then we were partners for seven years. However, you've got to be a little of each.

Q: Of the two types of big bands that we have throughout jazz history, the "hot" and the "sweet," yours had the reputation of being one of the leading "hot" bands. Did you plan it that way? Were you satisfied with the results?

Les: Well, you know we weren't necessarily considered a "hot" band, unless you're saying the "Mickey Mouse" bands were the sweet bands, and the swing bands were the "hot" bands. We were strictly a dance band. I had a very nice compliment come in by way of Sweden the other day. We're working on a tour of Scandinavia for this coming summer. It hasn't been finalized yet, and we don't even know if we're going to make it, but the guy that we got in touch with said, "Oh, yeah. Your band is the greatest dance band in the world." And we said, "But no jazz." And he said, "No, you're not the greatest jazz band, but you're the greatest dance band." There's a difference, though. They're altogether different. Like, Woody Herman, to me, as far as I'm concerned, has had the greatest jazz band that I've ever heard. I went up and was his master of ceremonies in Ventura about two or three weeks before he passed away, and I emceed part of the show. I never heard a band like that. I don't care, Ellington, Basie, anybody. I never heard a band as good as that.

Q: Your band's toured extensively from coast to coast, playing theaters, hotels, ballrooms, college campuses, and special events such as Bob Hope's annual tours. Why do you feel that touring gave your band the recognition to be one of the top bands in the country, rather than, say, staying out here in the Los Angeles area?

Les: Well, I don't agree that touring does that. I think in one television show, you'll hit many more people. In radio, you're exposed to more people in one radio shot than in a year of touring, if you have a coast-to-coast hook-up, which we did all the time. The only reason we went on tour was to make money. We went on tour, and we hated it. That's why we don't do it any more. We just did it to capitalize on all the air time we had, and the television time, and the exposure we had with Bob Hope. See, we've been with him since '47, so we've done both television and radio. You go on tour to make up the money you lost while you were sitting down.

Q: Of all the vocalists that worked with your band during its tenure, which ones do you feel had the qualities to enhance the musicality of your performances?

Les: Well, we've been lucky that way. We've had a lot of good vocalists, starting way back with Miriam Shaw, then Doris Day, Betty Bonny, and then Doris Day again, after she got her divorce and came back with the band, and Lucy Ann Polk. And on the men's side, we had Ray Kellogg and Jack Haskell. Another one we lost to the Hit Parade was Eileen Wilson. We lost her to the Hit Parade, but with my blessing, because she was a great singer, and we still hear from her now and then. Now we have Joanne Greer and Butch Stone. Butch Stone does more or less comedy work, and brother Stumpy does some rhythm work. I have my son singing with the band now, and he's sort of a Sinatra style. He phrases like Sinatra. I don't think he has his voice, but he sings in tune and he gets a lot of applause and recognition.

Q: What do you look for musically when you look for a singer?

Les: Well, voice first, and then intonation, which is very important. Without intonation you won't be there, that's all. I'd say that between Doris Day, Eileen Wilson, Joanne Greer and Lucy Ann Polk you had four different sounds but all of them good. They don't all have to sound like your favorite, whoever your favorite might be, whether it's Jo Stafford or Peggy Lee, or Doris Day, or whoever. There are different sounds, and they can all be good.

Q: What about the size of the bands? How have they changed during their development?

Les: When we started the Duke Blue Devils, we only had twelve pieces. We had one trombone, three trumpets and four saxes. Then we got five saxes and three trombones, and then four saxes and four trombones. Then we had a quartet, The Polka Dots. I was carrying about twenty-four people at one time. We're now back to a nice size of about seventeen.

Les Brown (Courtesy: Gene Howard, Les Brown Collection).

Q: Regarding the instrumentation, what made you go from two trumpets to three, to four, etc.?

Les: The competition. All the other bands had four trumpets and four trombones. Stan Kenton had five of each.

Q: It's generally accepted that the big band as an era ended during the late forties. Why did you feel this happened?

Les: Well, everything has to come to an end, even rock and roll may. In fact it has gone down hill and it's changed a lot. When Petrillo wouldn't let us record, right in the middle of the forties, the vocalists went ahead and recorded without his permission, because they didn't belong to his union. That hurt us a lot. However, we're doing a new album right now. We don't sell as much as we used to, but enough to pay the freight. The singers took over. Of course, we made the singers. The bands made the singers. We put them in front of the band, made heroes or heroines out of them, featured them and we improved ourselves right out of business.

Q: It's been said that history repeats itself. Every once in awhile you see a bumper sticker on a car that says, "Big Bands Are Back." What's your theory on that?

Les: Everybody says, "The big bands are coming back!" And I say "No, they're not. We don't have any ballrooms. That's where we played." There are no ballrooms left in the country worth talking about, maybe ten at the most, but only four or five would be major. We do concerts now and then. There's an interest in that. But, it's for people over forty-five, fifty, or sixty and seventy. Some of them are in their eighties.

Q: What is the style of your band today?

Les: I'd say ninety percent of our work is private parties. People say, "Where can we come to hear your band?" and I say, "Come to Disneyland next summer." That's open to the public. Now and then we play a concert that's open to the public, but most of our work is charity parties and weddings—not many weddings, maybe we play two or three a year. Because we play so many charity parties, we're putting some "yuppie" tunes in the books. I think they're the good ones, tunes that they like, not necessarily the Chubby Checker type of thing, but good ballads, like "We've Only Just Begun," "If," and "Evergreen."

Q: How do you compare the big band recording techniques of today with that during the thirties and forties?

Les: The last album we did is digital, which means, when you put it on a compact disc, you don't have to use a needle. It's the best sound we've ever gotten. We don't record much differently. We go in and record it all at once. We don't do like the small groups, or the contemporary groups that go in and lay down the rhythm track, then come in and put some violins above that. If they don't like the violins, they cut those out and put in trumpets instead, or trombones. If they don't like that, then they'll put in a synthesizer. We record the whole band. Then we get together and mix it. That's all. And we put a mike on every man in the band, which we didn't in the old days. We'd be lucky to have four mikes in the whole studio. We put a mike on every man in the band, and then when we mix it, if a guy hasn't played loud enough, we pull him up a little. If he played too loud, we pull him down a little. So, the final product will not be altogether the same as you heard on the "rough makes," as we call them.

Q: You hear a lot of live versus studio recordings by some of the bands. Have you been involved with live recordings?

Les: Probably our best album is a thing called "Concert at the Palladium," which was not a concert. That was the name of the album. We were at the Palladium for four weeks. We broadcast every night, and recorded every one of those broadcasts. Then we took the best of all those broadcasts and made an album out of them. It's not even stereo, because they didn't have stereo radio in those days. I think that's the best album we've ever done, and that's live, and non-stereo. That's when we had guys like Ronny Lang on alto sax, and Dave Pell on tenor. We had Ray Sims, Zoot's brother, on trombone, who played so beautifully. We had

Don Fagerquist on trumpet, Jack Sperling, whom we still have on the drums, and Tony Reesie on guitar; Jeff Clarks on the piano. That was a great band, too. And that was never mixed, couldn't be mixed. The only thing we did if we had a bad broadcast, or a bad number on a broadcast, was to eliminate it.

Q: About recordings, were they influential in setting the styles of the big bands during the thirties and forties?

Les: Well, of course. If you didn't have records, you better forget it. And that's what's happening today. You know, there are probably more big bands around today than ever. Every college has one, and a lot of high schools have one, and damn good ones, too. But, they don't make records. I mean they don't make records that are open to the public, and you don't have a public that's buying that kind of record nowadays. So you might as well say they don't exist. It's like the tree that falls in the forest. If there's nobody around to hear it, it didn't fall. That's what's happening. If you don't record, forget it.

Q: Regarding all the different names associated with bands, such as Guy Lombardo's Royal Canadians, Lawrence Welk's Champagne Music, Harry James' Music Makers. How did you get the name, ''The Band of Renown''?

Les: In 1942 we were at the Hotel Roosevelt in Washington D.C., and we had a wire. We were supposed to broadcast at ten o'clock at night. Anyway, it came time for the broadcast, and we had a theme that had a trombone solo in it. Si Zentner, who was our first trombone player, wasn't on the bandstand. We sent Butch Dolman out and he looked around and found Si, got him by the ear, and pulled him on the bandstand. In the meantime, the announcer was stretching, and stretching, and stretching. When I finally gave him the signal to go, he said, ''And here's the band of renown, Les Brown!'' Thank God that Si was off the bandstand, because we picked that up, and have used it ever since.

Q: Your theme song is titled ''Leap Frog.'' Who wrote it, where did you find it, and why did you adopt that as your musical logo?

Les: I guess it was at a two-week session at the Hotel Roosevelt. We had been carrying ''Leap Frog'' around in a suitcase for over a year before we had a chance to rehearse it. We finally had a rehearsal, because we were going to the Palladium right after that, in June of 1942. We had a rehearsal and tried ''Leap Frog,'' and we loved it so much we threw the old theme away. We used ''Leap Frog'' from then on. It was written by Joe Garland, who also wrote ''In the Mood'' for Glenn Miller.

Q: When you get a new arrangement, how do you decide its structure?

Les: I've had, at different times, different arrangers. Ben Holburn and I did the arranging back in the 40's. Then Frank Comstock joined us, and Skip Martin, and Jay Hill for the last 30 years. Skip, like Frank Comstock, played with the band, so he knew what I wanted. In the same way, Jay Hill played trombone with the band, and he knew what I wanted. They tailor-made them for the band we happened to have. We have arrangements that I can't use because the band I have now doesn't fit the arrangements that were made back in the forties and fifties. They just don't fit, so we don't use them.

Q: Has the style changed that much?

Les: Not so much the style as the men. Arrangements were tailor-made for the men we had at that time. The strengths and the weaknesses change. We have so many arrangements. We're up into the four thousand numbers now.

Q: What about guitars? Do you use a guitar in your rhythm section?

Les: Not anymore. However, we do when we record.

Q: Do both piano and guitar seem to perform the same basic functions?

Les: The piano isn't a rhythm instrument. Piano's a solo instrument.

Q: When you have a three-man rhythm section; piano, bass and drums, how then do you regard the piano?

Les: When you don't have the guitar, piano does help in the rhythm section. Like Basie—if he played a hundred notes a night, he got overtime, but he had a great guitarist in Freddy Green. When we record, the piano doesn't work as a rhythm instrument. It just plays solos and fills.

Q: Regarding the sidemen, soloists, and leadmen, what training, education, and experience do you expect of them before you hire them on your band?

Les: Just that they play well, that's all. Play well, play in tune, have a good tone, and keep their nose clean. Don't drink too much, and things like that. If we lose a man, we have to think of the arrangements that we are currently using, so we have to hire a man that fits the same category.

Q: How about high tech electronics? Has that affected style, performance, and the audience expectations of jazz, in relation to the big bands?

Les: Some big bands might use an electronic keyboard. In fact, we're thinking of doing that, because we hit too many pianos that are out of tune. You know, you go into a hotel and they say, ''Well, we had it tuned last fall.'' They think that once a year is enough, or something like that. We play for so many private parties. We don't blow them out of the room, or they don't have us back. There are a few bands that have made that mistake, right here in L.A., and thanks to them, we're getting more work.

Q: How does the jazz style of your band compare with the overall big band style of some of the other bands? Do you try to make it distinctive, so they know this is the Les Brown sound, compared to the Basie sound or the Ellington sound?

Les: According to what people tell me, we have evolved some kind of a Les Brown sound. They say, ''We can tell your band right away.'' I wish I could. We don't have anything that's instantaneously recognizable. For example, when Billy May came out with a band, you could tell right from the intro who it was. You could always tell when it was Guy Lombardo. They were identifiable. We don't have anything in our sound that does that. I think it takes a musician to tell whether it's our band or, say, Ray Anthony.

Q: What do you feel is the future for women instrumentalists in jazz?

Les: Great, if they can play. I don't know if there's any future in it. They have to really love it to want to travel like they do. If they can play and have the stamina, it would be fine. I've never had one that's asked for a job in my band. I never gave it a thought. I know Woody had a girl for awhile. I met a Japanese girl in Tokyo back in 1950. Today she's a fine arranger and bandleader. Her name is Toshiko Akiyoshi. When I met her, she was in her teens. We were in Japan with Bob Hope during the Korean War. She was performing at the Deichi Hotel. We went in to hear her and one of our party asked her to sing something. She sang, note for note, one of Dizzy Gillespie's solos with perfect pitch. Then about eight or ten years later, I was in New York and I went to the Hickory House on Fifty-second Street. There's a Japanese girl playing piano, and playing very well, by the way. At the end of her set, she comes by and says, ''Hello, Mr. Brown.'' I asked her how she knew me and she says, ''I know you by your records and I met you at the Deichi Hotel in Tokyo.'' She had gone to Berklee in Boston. She is a great musician. Now, if I could find a few like that, I'd have them on the band anytime.

Q: What advice do you have for young jazz musicians wanting to make music a career?

Les: Well, again, you'd better be the best or forget it. You've got to be right on top or love it that much that you can't be happy any other way, because it's pretty hard to make a living financially as a musician. Even the best men here in Los Angeles right now are having a hard time getting by, because like Petrillo said, "You're going to record yourself out of business." And I think we have.

Q: What personal satisfaction do you get from performing, both as an instrumentalist yourself, and as a leader?

Les: I haven't played enough to talk about in the last twenty, twenty-five years. I don't play solos or anything anymore. I do play with the saxophone section now and then, only because I have an instrument and I keep it in shape, and I guess I think it looks good, or something. But, I do enjoy conducting. I did ten years of conducting on the Dean Martin show, and that takes conducting. You don't just say "one, two, three, four," and go. And, of course, I've been with Bob Hope conducting for forty-one years. I get a good deal of satisfaction from that.

Q: What do you think has happened to jazz over the past forty years?

Les: Well, I don't think the big bands have changed that much, but of course it went into bop and then all kinds of jazz, from West coast, East coast, Latin. There's been some very interesting innovations, I'd say.

Q: What gave you the biggest satisfaction of being a big band leader over a long and illustrious career?

Les: Being successful, for one. Well, I got lucky. When I joined Bob Hope we settled down in California and we've been here ever since. What little traveling we've done since 1947 was minimal.

Q: Are the kids today better prepared on their instruments than was the case thirty or forty years ago?

Les: I'd say there are more good musicians around now than ever, and it's such a shame that they can't get a decent job. Woody had a pipeline to the best. I never heard kids like that play so well. And I say kids, because I don't believe there's anybody in the band except Frank Tiberi, the leader, and the road manager who is over thirty. Everybody else is anywhere from nineteen up, and they are wonderful. They are virtuosos.

Q: Who, in your opinion, had the greatest single influence on the development of big band jazz?

Les: Well, I'd say Fletcher Henderson, with his arrangements. As soon as I heard Benny Goodman play those Fletcher Henderson arrangements, my whole idea about big band swing changed. And, of course, all the great arrangements of Count Basie.

Q: What do you think's going to happen in the future for the big bands?

Les: Well, once the leader passes away, it's not the same. You can't tell me the Duke Ellington band is like it used to be. You can't tell me the Count Basie band is like it used to be. And let's face it. It's a financial thing. The lawyers that own the Glenn Miller band were thinking of putting out a second unit of the Glenn Miller band. I don't think it happened, and I don't think it will. The Glenn Miller name is so legendary and so famous. You know he's been dead forty-four years. He had a very popular band, and he made a lot of good records.

Q: What leisure time activity do you enjoy?

Les: Well, I used to enjoy golf. I'm down to about once a week on golf now, because I'm playing so poorly. I'm embarrassed to get out there, but I still like the walk in the park. I do play bridge at least four or five times a week. That takes care of my leisure time, except reading. When we finish the evening news and have our dinner, we go to bed and read until 10:00 or 10:30, and then turn out the light.

Les Brown Band of Renown at the Carnation Plaza, Disneyland. (Courtesy of R. Gaynor).

Les Brown Band of Renown Recordings:

Les Brown Concert Modern	Capital	T959
Dance to South Pacific	Capital	T1060
Les Brown Bandland	Columbia	CC 1497
Les Brown The Band of Renown Plays the Gershwin Bandbook	Columbia	CS 8479
Les Brown Goes Direct to Disc	Century Records	CRDD 1010

Chapter 4
The Big Bands Play On

Dr. Gene Aitken

Because of the negative connotation associated with the title "Ghost Bands," we will simply call them today's big bands. These bands are currently led by someone other than the original leader whose name remains associated with the band. The band still tours, uses the name of the original leader and, in most cases, spends a majority of its time on the road as in the past. The new leaders now fronting the bands come from a variety of backgrounds. New leaders may have played in the original band, gained the original leader's respect for their musicianship, or taken on the leadership through a business agreement with the original leader or individuals in charge of the estate.

What about some of the famous road bands such as Stan Kenton, Don Ellis and Buddy Rich that are no longer performing? Usually the individuals specified in their wills that the bands would not continue with their names. In most cases the band's music is given to colleges or universities to archive for educational and research purposes. The reason for this approach is usually personal, as the original leader wanted the band to be remembered for what it was.

Road bands were born out of several concepts. First, those persons who inherited the estate of a big band wish to see the name continued or wish to continue playing as members of the band. They negotiate with an interested new leader and/or sideman and work out a financial and artistic agreement to put the band back on the road. This may happen immediately or it may take years. Another way the bands continue is to have someone front the band when the leader

Dr. Gene Aitken

retires. The original leader maintains some artistic control or is at least informed about the band's progress and schedule. Finally, road bands are formed by an agency at the request of relatives who relinquish control to the agency.

There does not seem to be the opportunities for road bands today that there were in prior years. Part of the problem is the prevalence of television in the home and also the demands of work and commuting during the week. People tend not to go out during the week. This makes it extremely difficult for the road bands to exist, as most must work every night to make the tour financially sound. An additional factor which makes it difficult for road bands is that record companies are not recording the established road bands as they had done in the past. The results are two-fold: road bands do not receive exposure because there is no new album release advertising, and radio play is limited due to the lack of interest. Thus big bands as an entertainment commodity are not being marketed.

Today, musicians in most of the road bands are college graduates. This is a change from past years when most musicians received their "education" on the road. Many colleges boast of their graduates who are now or have been performing with some of these bands.

Most leaders today agree that the quality of musicians is generally improved. They have both the technical ability and the musicianship to fit in with the band after a few rehearsals or performances. These musicians have a good understanding of basic musical fundamentals and style.

Most leaders generally agree that the young musicians today should go to a good college and obtain a degree before going on the road. This avenue seems to produce better musicians and places them in performance situations where they can be heard. It is important that good basic musical fundamentals are learned, as the competition is strenuous. The musician should play in as many different situations as possible, including classical, Dixieland, big bands, combos, "top 40" bands, etc. Most road bands today are primarily made up of college graduates who are twenty-two to twenty-five years of age. They are individuals who are serious about making music for a living.

Although there are few actively touring road bands, musicians who travel with a road band gain a wealth of on-the-job training. These are situations where young musicians can receive money for something they love to do . . . playing music. The musicians are learning to work together while playing on a regular basis and receiving a living wage. They are exchanging and sharing musical ideas and learning to be consistent under many different acoustical conditions. Being around a high level of musicianship seems to make each musician perform better. Other benefits include learning a style of music and improving their playing.

How are new members selected? A few band leaders will listen to every audition tape that comes in, but will then give the tape to the section leader for final recommendation. Other leaders do not have the time to listen to tapes and will pass the tape directly to the section leader. The most difficult method of getting a job in road bands today is arranging a live audition in a city where the road band is performing. Most musicians are tired and prefer to rest rather than listen to auditions.

In most cases, the section leader will make the final recommendation, and the leader will concur. As in the past, though guided by the leader, most of the personnel decisions remain with the band's members. It is important for the musicians to feel they have input concerning the quality of their members.

In about ninety-nine percent of the cases, a musician in the band knows or has heard of someone who is a good player. "Word of mouth," jam sessions, hearing other professional or college bands and recommendations of respected alumni seem to be the best methods of getting a road job today.

Traveling on the road in the 1980's is much easier due to interstate highways and improved transportation and travel conditions. Bands can get to engagements faster and easier than in the 1940's. Performances for most bands are also shorter, with the average performance, concert or dance being only two to three hours in length.

With few exceptions today, leaders of the road bands open and close a concert or dance with the theme song of the original leader. The majority of the music performed is the band's original music. Most new leaders realize the importance of updating their repertoires to include current hits.

Today's Bands

Some road bands work on an occasional basis within a small geographic area in order to keep the same personnel. The musicians in these bands usually maintain a full-time job, raise a family and still enjoy music-making part-time.

For road bands that are committed to touring a wider geographic area on a full-time basis, not much has changed over the years. The average tenure for these musicians seems to be about two years. The reasons for leaving are varied—to start a family, to go back to their family and to go with other bands. Others tire of the road and seek out studio jobs or work with smaller groups in the more populated cities. Many musicians' tenure is shorter if they don't meet the musical requirements of the group or if they do not relate to other musicians. Tenure has been known to be as short as one tune.

With few exceptions, women instrumentalists are discouraged by most band leaders from becoming members of road bands. The road is hard and long, and problems of sharing rooms are both real and expensive. In most bands, musicians must pay for their own room costs. Therefore, musicians double and triple up to save money. In a few bands, the management may pay for amounts over "x" dollars. This allows the musicians to have individual rooms which makes traveling much easier. A woman singer may be important for the success of the band, in situations where the agency budgets and pays the additional expense.

Nine of the most noted bands are described here. Even in the word descriptions, the character of each as an individual group is evident from its leadership, instrumentation, music, and performance schedule.

The Count Basie Orchestra

After Count Basie died in April 1984, Eric Dixon acted as interim director until a permanent one was selected. In 1985, trumpeter Thad Jones took over the leadership of the band. From late 1986 on, tenor saxophonist Frank Foster has been the leader of this orchestra. Both Thad Jones and Frank Foster were members of the band for an extended period of time.

In 1935, the Count Basie Orchestra grew out of Benny Moten's orchestra after Benny died. The band has been touring steadily ever since, with Kansas City as their original home base. They have remained at the top of their craft with artists, critics and musicians. The Basie Orchestra is one of the few bands that has backed many of the great singers including Jimmy Rushing, Joe Williams, Helen Humes, Ella Fitzgerald, Sarah Vaughn, Frank Sinatra, Tony Bennett and others. The band tours approximately forty weeks each year, with several of those weeks spent in Japan and/or Europe. A majority of the performances are concerts rather than dances. Count Basie admitted that the sound of the tenor saxophone had special excitement for him. That is why the band has been built from the rhythm section to the tenor saxophone. One only has to acknowledge tenor saxophonists such as Lester Young, Illinois Jacquet, Paul Gonsalves, Lucky Thompson, Ben Webster, Frank Foster and Frank Wess who served with the Basie band to be aware of Basie's special interest in that instrument.

Frank Foster, leader, The Count Basie Orchestra (Courtesy: Thomas Cassidy, Artist Management).

The instrumentation of the band remains the same, with four trumpets, four trombones, five saxophones, piano, bass, guitar, and drums. The Basie Orchestra is one of few established groups that does not use a theme song. The tunes most requested are "Corner Pocket," "In a Mellow Tone," "Wind Machine," "Strike Up the Band," "Easy Living" and "Booty's Blues."

The Xavier Cugat Orchestra

The Xavier Cugat Orchestra has been together for approximately two and one-half years touring in the New York area. They are currently working quite steadily at the Roseland Ballroom and have toured to both Disneyland and Disney World. The orchestra is now under the leadership of Ada Cavallo, the only new female leader of an established road band. Xavier Cugat, who was eighty-eight years old on January 1, 1988, retired the original orchestra approximately twenty years ago. The 1984 Presidential Inaugural Ball Committee requested that Mr. Cugat bring a group to Washington D.C. for a special performance. Through Mr. Cugat's brother Enric Cugat, Ada Cavallo was given the rights to re-establish the orchestra for seven years with an option to continue. Although Ms. Cavallo and her pianist husband, Bob Kasha, had not performed with the band, they did study the music and receive input from both of the Cugats. Xavier Cugat receives tapes of the group's performances and is kept up to date on the schedule.

Ada, who is from the Dominican Republic, is a superb performer and sings in five different languages. Performing one of the standard Cugat tunes like "Cumbanchero" is very natural. Prior to her association with the Cugat Orchestra, she performed regularly with Bob Hope and Chucky Green.

Most of the musicians in the group today are the top players in the New York area. Because of this, the price to contract the orchestra is relatively high. The same musicians are employed for every performance/dance and although not working every night, the band does keep busy for approximately ten months of the year. The instrumentation, fifteen in all, consists of three trumpets, one trombone, four saxophones, piano, bass, drums, marimba, conga drums/timbales and two women singers/dancers, one of whom is Ada.

Ada Cavallo, leader, The Xavier Cugat Orchestra (Courtesy: Thomas Cassidy, Artist Management).

The opening and closing theme song of the Xavier Cugat Orchestra is "My Shawl." "My Shawl" was the first tune Frank Sinatra recorded. It was recorded with the Xavier Cugat Orchestra. In addition to this popular tune, the Xavier Cugat Orchestra was identified with such tunes as "Tico Tico" featuring Carmen Miranda, "Brazil," "Siboney" and "Two Hearts that Pass in the Night." The other music played by the orchestra combines the best of the nostalgic feeling with today's style. The group plays music that is considered very melodic, yet commercial. One can relax to the music, dance to it, and have fun with it.

The Jimmy Dorsey Orchestra

The Jimmy Dorsey Orchestra has been under the direction of Lee Castle since 1957. Lee is considered by many leaders and musicians to have had the longest, steadiest career of any musician on the road. He began with Tommy Dorsey in 1938, and then went with the bands of Artie Shaw, Benny Goodman, Glenn Miller and others. He then formed his own band. When Tommy and Jimmy Dorsey merged in 1953, Lee gave up his band and became the featured trumpeter and music director. When Tommy Dorsey died, it became the Jimmy Dorsey Band. When Jimmy died, Lee Castle assumed the leadership of the Jimmy Dorsey Band. The band is on the road approximately forty weeks a year. Most of the jobs are one-nighters, with an occasional location date. Although Lee tries to keep the same personnel, the band does add new musicians. When new persons join the group, the basic goal is for them to understand the style ... it's not the notes, but what one does with them.

The instrumentation is the same as in the original band; three trumpets, three trombones, five saxophones, piano, bass, drums and the leader. The band opens and closes each performance with the theme song, "Contrasts." The Jimmy Dorsey Band was also identified with "So Rare" and "Jay-Dee's Boogie Woogie."

Lee Castle, leader, The Jimmy Dorsey Orchestra (Courtesy: Thomas Cassidy, Artist Management).

The Tommy Dorsey Orchestra

Buddy Morrow, leader, The Tommy Dorsey Orchestra (Courtesy: Thomas Cassidy, Artist Management).

The Tommy Dorsey Orchestra is now under the leadership of Buddy Morrow (since April 1977), who was with the original band in 1937–38. He has been with the bands of Eddie Duchin, Artie Shaw, Vincent Lopez, Jimmy Dorsey and others. For several years he fronted his own band and in 1952 recorded "Night Train," which hit the top of the charts and is still popular.

The band is on the road approximately forty-five weeks a year, with a majority of the engagements being one-nighters. The crowds come primarily to dance to old familiar tunes. Approximately seventy-five percent of the music played is original Dorsey music. The library is updated only if it fits the style. The instrumentation of the band is the same as that of the original band; four trumpets, four trombones, five saxophones, piano, bass, drums and a male singer. In the Golden Years of the Forties, musicians such as Buddy Rich, Frank Sinatra and Ziggy Elman were members of this band.

The theme song, "I'm Getting Sentimental Over You," is played at the beginning and ending of each performance. In addition, the tunes that the original Tommy Dorsey Orchestra made famous are played—"I'll Never Smile Again," "Once In A While," "Opus No. 1," "Marie," "The Song of India" and many more.

The Duke Ellington Orchestra

Mercer Ellington, leader, The Duke Ellington Orchestra (Courtesy: Carl Schunk and Associates).

Duke Ellington began his orchestra in 1925 in the New York area. The group has never stopped, thus making it the oldest continuing orchestra, now in its seventh decade. Although not a large ensemble in the beginning, as Duke heard good players and the potential for a new sound or flavor in the band, he would add musicians, rather than replace them. As an example, Duke started with four saxophone players, Johnny Hodges, Otto Hardwicke, Barney Bigard and Harry Carney. Then when he became aware of Ben Webster, rather than fire anyone, Ben was added. The new member then would have to play by ear while the others were playing music that had been put down for them. A lot of the music that was performed by Duke's band was never written down. "Rockin' In Rhythm," "Perdido" and "Caravan" are a few examples.

When Duke died, May 25, 1974, the band performed in honor of him for the next six months or so. The orchestra kept receiving requests, and thus the band continued. His son, Mercer Ellington, who had performed with the band as early as 1927, played trombone with the orchestra in the 1950's. Then, later in the 1960's, he rejoined the band as a member of the trumpet section.

The band, which received a Grammy in 1988, is very religious about performing the music exactly as Duke had written it. New music is being written for the orchestra, in addition to music composed by Duke that has never been performed by the orchestra. As an example, some music scheduled for the next album was written by Duke for Haile Selassie (1892-1975), Emperor of Ethiopia.

The performances of the Ellington Orchestra are about half dances and half concerts. The instrumentation stayed as Duke had it; five saxophones, four trumpets, three trombones, piano, bass, drums and Mercer leading the orchestra. At church engagements, a synthesizer and an extra drummer may be added. Although there is no theme song per se, the band does open each performance with "A Train." Other tunes that are popular are "Mood Indigo," "Sophisticated Lady," "Satin Doll," "Do Nothing 'Til You Hear From Me" and "I Got It Bad and That Ain't Good."

Over the years the band has developed some outstanding musicians. Kenny Garrett, alto saxophonist who was with the Ellington Band, is now with Miles Davis. Mulgrew Miller, pianist, is now a shining star in the jazz field.

The orchestra tours the entire year, as much as fifty weeks. Although a majority of the engagements are one-nighters, the band also performs about twenty-two sacred concerts annually.

The Woody Herman Band

Frank Tiberi, leader, The Woody Herman Band (Courtesy: Thomas Cassidy, Artist Management).

The Woody Herman Band is unique in that its leader, Frank Tiberi, and road manager, Bill Byrne, have been with the band over twenty years. Frank Tiberi was forty-two when he started touring with Woody's band in 1969. Prior to that time, he attended Curtis School of music, studied classical bassoon and worked as a free-lance saxophonist. Bill Byrne, who attended the Cincinnati Conservatory and the U.S. Naval Academy, eventually went to New York and played in Larry Elgart's band for about a year. In 1965, Woody was looking for three trumpet players. Bill Byrne has been with the band ever since.

Woody Herman ran his band much differently than most others. He always had writer-musicians in the band composing or arranging for the players. It helped to keep the spirit up in the band, because the band constantly had new arrangements that reflected its current personality.

The band is on the road approximately forty weeks a year, averaging six nights a week. Years ago, the majority of the performances were dance jobs for Elks clubs, Moose clubs, etc. Today, the majority of the performances are high school and college concerts. The Woody Herman Band is one of the few organizations that encouraged women to travel with the band, from vocalist Mary Ann McCall in 1937 and trumpeter Billie Roger in 1942, to pianist Janis Friedman today.

The theme song the Woody Herman Band uses to open and close performances is "Blue Flame." Other tunes that Woody's band made famous were "Caldonia," "Four Brothers," "Woodchoppers Ball," "Early Autumn," and "Bijou."

The Harry James Orchestra

Joe Graves, leader, The Harry James Orchestra (Courtesy: Thomas Cassidy, Artist Management).

The original Harry James Orchestra began in 1939 and was active on the road until he died in July, 1983. The five years prior to his death, Harry James was quite ill. Intent on continuing the band so musicians would not be put out of work, Harry had heard the Time/Life Record Series Joe Graves recorded. He recommended to Pee Wee Monte, owner and manager of the Harry James Orchestra, that Joe be given the opportunity to lead the band. By March, 1984, trumpeter Joe Graves, who had played with the James Orchestra in the mid-1940's, was fronting the band. Joe's background included playing with most of the big bands such as Jimmy and Tommy Dorsey, Benny Goodman, Charlie Barnett, Bob Crosby, Ray Noble, etc. Joe had worked all the recording studios in Los Angeles and from 1966 to 1979 worked in the Las Vegas house bands.

The band today, which works out of Los Angeles, plays cruise ships and engagements on the West Coast. Rather than work on a regular touring schedule such as "weeks-per-year" basis, they work three or four nights a week and sometimes none. Personnel stays very steady due to the limited touring schedule, which allows the musicians to do studio work and other jobs. Most of the band members today are musicians who worked with Harry James. The musicians are very loyal and check with the management before taking other offers.

The instrumentation of the band has stayed the same; four trumpets, three trombones, five saxes, piano, bass, drums, a female singer and Joe Graves, leader. Most of the engagements are dances rather than concerts. A shortened theme song, "Ciribiribin," is played at the beginning and ending of each performance. The tunes which Harry James was noted for include "You Made Me Love You," his biggest seller, "Cherry," "Sleepy Lagoon" and "Two 'O Clock Jump." A majority of the hits were ballads, although they were rarely played on the road. Today, the band plays the book as it was when Harry James was with the band. No new, updated tunes are added. There are approximately 2,500 tunes in the library, many of which were not played before.

The Glenn Miller Orchestra

Glenn Miller's Orchestra, which was disbanded in 1944 when Glenn Miller's plane disappeared over the English Channel, was re-formed in 1956 by Helen Miller, Glenn's widow, and Dave McKay, Sr. The orchestra, which has had six major leaders, was led by drummer Ray McKinley until 1964. At that time, clarinetist Buddy DeFranco took over for ten years until 1974. During the next several months there were a number of short-term leaders. Toward the end of 1974 and into 1975, trombonist Buddy Morrow assumed the leadership. Trombonist Jimmy Henderson headed up the orchestra from 1975 until 1981. More recently, from 1981 until 1983, the group was directed by trombonist Larry O'Brien. Since 1983, the band has been under the leadership of tenor saxophonist Dick Gerhart.

Today, the Glenn Miller Orchestra is under the management of Dave McKay, Jr., the operating head of Glenn Miller Productions which owns and operates the group. Although there is only one official Glenn Miller Orchestra, there are times when some of the former band's alumni are assembled to do a special date because the touring Glenn Miller Orchestra is committed.

The band currently tours approximately forty-eight weeks a year, with approximately twelve to fifteen weeks overseas. Although it is not an easy lifestyle, the majority of the engagements are one-night stands. Location dates are becoming increasingly scarce, and most of those are overseas. The instrumentation of the band has remained the same over the years: the leader, male and female singers, four trumpets, four trombones, five saxes, piano, bass and drums for a total of nineteen musicians.

As in the days when Glenn Miller fronted the band, the opening and closing theme of the Glenn Miller Orchestra is "Moonlight Serenade." The most requested tunes are "Little Brown Jug," "Pennsylvania 6-5000," "In the Mood," "Elmer's Tune," "Chattanooga Choo-Choo" and "Kalamazoo." In addition to the male and female singers, the leader and a couple of the musicians form a singing group, the "Moonlight Serenaders."

Although there are over seventeen hundred tunes from the original book, the band does add contemporary tunes in the Glenn Miller style. Tunes such as "I Sing the Body Electric," from *Fame*, and "Can You Read My Mind?" from *Superman*, are examples of music that has been added to the library.

The Artie Shaw Orchestra

The Artie Shaw Orchestra was disbanded in 1976 and re-established in 1984 under the leadership of clarinetist Dick Johnson. Mr. Johnson's background was primarily with Benny Goodman, Buddy Morrow, and other bands. He has recorded with pianist Dave McKenna for Concord Records and appeared as a guest artist at the Monterey Jazz Festival with the Woody Herman Band.

When the band reorganized, Artie Shaw rehearsed them. He now goes out with the band once or twice a year. The first year the band was on the road, they were out seventeen weeks. They could have been on the road approximately twenty-five weeks, but in order to keep the same top musicians (most of them studio players from Boston), the leader was sensitive to their professional and social commitments and chose the shorter schedule.

The instrumentation (five saxophones, four trumpets, three trombones, four-man rhythm section, with Dick Johnson up front), is the same as when Artie Shaw was leading the band. The majority of their dates are one-nighters, with a week or two a year at Disneyland and/or Disney World.

Dick Johnson, leader, The Artie Shaw Orchestra (Courtesy: Thomas Cassidy, Artist Management).

The band's theme song is "Nightmare," a slow and haunting melody which is played at the beginning and ending of each performance. Songs that are most requested are Artie Shaw's two big hits, "Begin the Beguine" and "Carioca."

How Are Bands Employed Today?

Assisted by a few key agencies/management people like Tom Cassidy of Tom Cassidy Artists' Management (Woodstock, Illinois); Wayne Hutchinson (New York); Bob Bonis of the Phoenix Talent Agency (Great Neck, New York); VIN Attractions (New York); Dave McKay of Glenn Miller Productions (New York); Bill Curtis (Boston, Massachusetts); Pee Wee Monte (Los Angeles) and the Count Basie Enterprises, Inc. (New York), road bands are able to keep nearly full schedules. Sonny Anderson, who is connected with Walt Disney World, Epcot Center and Disneyland, is instrumental in bringing big bands to these areas for several summer evening concerts. As a result, thousands of big-band enthusiasts are able to listen to the music of these great bands.

Future

Most new leaders agree that the number of road bands is steadily decreasing. There are areas of the country, however, where there is tremendous support for road bands. For the last forty years, band leaders have predicted that road bands would not continue to exist, yet those that continue do stay busy.

Dr. Gene Aitken—Biography

Dr. Gene Aitken is director of Jazz Studies at the University of Northern Colorado, and is associate director of the L.A. Jazz Workshops in Los Angeles. In these capacities, he spends a large amount of time as a commuter between California and Colorado.

At the author's request, he has created this chapter on the Big Bands of the thirties and forties, many of which are still performing nationwide under new leadership, since many of the original leaders have either retired or passed away. In any event, the new leaders have retained the format and style of the original band and enhanced it by adding new dimensions in sound and instrumentation. Many of the band personnel in today's bands were not even born when these bands were at their peak during the big band era.

Dr. Aitken has researched this subject in great depth by interviewing many of the parties involved with the bands. He feels that while the era of the big bands has long since ended, many of the styles and sounds and traditions continue to exist.

In his position as Director of Jazz Studies, Dr. Aitken has developed one of the leading collegiate jazz programs in the country. Not just offering programs in big band and small band jazz groups, he has also developed a vocal jazz program, the recordings of which have been nominated for Grammys. In addition, the Los Angeles based vocal jazz group Terra Nova, which coached by Aitken, won the 1986 Hennessey-Playboy Jazz Search and appeared at the opening of the 1986 Playboy Jazz Festival at the Hollywood Bowl. His UNC-Greeley Jazz Festival is rated as one of the most prestigious jazz events for colleges and universities in the nation.

An excellent jazz bassist, he has appeared on performances with, Mel Torme, Vicki Carr, The Four Freshmen, Si Zentner, Les Elgart and many more. He is one of the most sought after clinicians for vocal and instrumental clinics and jazz festivals.

Otto Werner

Chapter 5
Women in Jazz

Women in jazz have made valuable contributions to its development through the eras and even as far back as its African roots. Today, in large part due to music programs both in high schools and colleges throughout the country, women are playing a very active role. Women are singers with bands and instrumentalists as well. The area of jazz in which there seems to be rather limited female activity is that of composition and arranging. Exceptions in this area include bandleader, pianist, composer/arranger Toshiko Akiyoshi, from Japan, who, along with her saxophonist husband, Lew Tabackin, have been favorites among audiences in this country and Japan for several years. Her published band arrangements have become standard literature with school jazz bands.

"The problem with women jazz musicians is that they simply cannot make the music swing." So stated a leading authority on jazz a number of years ago. And that concept has not changed appreciably in recent years. Although strides have been made to disprove that statement, women are still a minority in the professional world of jazz. "They have been used out of necessity, to add a bit of charm and glamour to an otherwise unattractive body of persons in the beings of the jazz musicians with wrinkled and unkempt attire and general slovenly appearance, and little or no personal pride in grooming." That, too, is an ill-conceived

Lew Tabackin (left) and Toshiko Akiyoshi, bandleaders (Courtesy: Thomas Cassidy, Artist Management).

generalization. Society has often stereotyped the jazz musician as anything but a stalwart citizen. The life-style was seen as one with booze, drugs, and tobacco. The musician had few roots and no direction in life other than playing jazz in some hovel called a nightclub. Both these views are erroneous.

Women have been successful in making a contribution to the development of jazz. Individual women are recognized for this contribution. In some comparisons, their contributions far exceed that in other fields—politics and major league sports, to name only two. The purpose of this chapter is to recognize the accomplishments of some of these women. Exploration into the lives of individual personalities can serve as inspiration and provide lessons for greater equality of opportunity for all in jazz.

Historically, women in the African tribes played an active role in tribal music. While men played the percussion instruments, the women adeptly performed on the kalimba, also known as the thumb piano. This instrument was constructed in a box-like fashion similar to the guitar, with a tone hole over which was placed a series of springs which were plucked with the fingers. Small in size (6" x 10" to 8" x 10") it projected the sound quite well over the playing of the drums. The flutes and lutes were also played by women. Women were largely responsible for singing the songs of the tribe. The voice ranges of the women gave them much better projection than the men. In a time without sound reinforcement, effective projection was a necessity.

During the era of slavery and the work song, the woman's voice again was essential to make the songs heard above the instrumental accompaniments. It may be the quality of the female voice and the projection ability that made it a popular addition to the evolution of jazz, from the work song through today. The male voice also contributed to the development of jazz. A large number of male singers were and still are active performers either as solo song stylists or as members of bands. In early jazz, following the abolition of slavery, women were involved in minstrel shows as singers with the emphasis being on songs of the blues. Bessie Smith was a member of a minstrel troupe prior to becoming a solo singer and recording artist on the T.O.B.A. circuit. Gertrude "Ma" Rainey was the first women bandleader of any renown. Married to "Pa" Rainey, she was a singer in his band prior to forming her own Georgia Jazz Band, although in this capacity, she was a singer and not an instrumentalist.

Of the women instrumentalists, Lillian Hardin (later to become Mrs. Louis Armstrong) was a pianist in a New York City music store. Her assignment was to play sheet music for customers who wanted to hear the piano arrangement prior to deciding whether or not to purchase it. (George Gershwin had a similar job many years later in a music store in the same city.) It was while she held this job that Louis Armstrong, then a member of the King Oliver band, was in New York and visited the music store where he met Ms. Hardin. Their friendship culminated in marriage. She so impressed King Oliver with her musical ability that he hired her as the pianist with his band. She later became the pianist with several other Dixieland bands, including Armstrong's Hot Five and Hot Seven. Of her many compositions, the best known is "Struttin' With Some Barbecue." Louis claimed authorship of it and had his name placed on the music as the composer. Following their divorce many years later, she successfully sued Louis for title as the songwriter, and was paid a large amount of back royalties. Today, her name justly appears as the song's composer. It has become one of the classic standards of Dixieland music.

While Lil Hardin was very popular performing with an all-male band, a number of women were involved as members and featured soloists with all-female bands. Their territory was primarily as featured attractions on the Keith and Orpheum circuits during vaudeville. These bands appeared in shows as accompaniment for singers and dancers as well as having their own special places on the program. Women jazz instrumentalists, as well as singers, were to be found in the casts of Florenz Ziegfield's annual Follies and George White's Scandals. Both men changed stage shows each year during the Twenties, featuring new acts and individuals. Drummer/entertainer Ann Pennington was an excellent musician and appeared in the Ziegfield Follies of 1924, during which she was rated as one of the highest paid stars in all of entertainment.

Other female instrumentalists who were popular during the Twenties deserve mention. Bess Vance, drummer, played with Harry Waiman's Debutantes on the Orpheum Circuit. Gene Peterson, saxophonist/xylophonist also nicknamed the "musical doll," appeared with her group at the Bamboo Inn in Indianapolis. Ms. Percy Nolan, a dance band drummer with the Burch orchestra, played the territory in and around Seattle. Elsie Perry was the drummer/leader/manager of the Ladies' Nonpareil Orchestra in Circleville, New York. She was also the secretary of local 819 of the Musicians' Union, a position normally held by a man. Peggy Steele played the vaudeville circuits with Grace Simpson's Melody Girls and then became the leader of her own band, called the Mayflower band, which headquartered in New Haven, Connecticut. Mary Zoller, a vibraphonist, was one of the first instrumentalists to popularize the instrument with which Lionel Hampton became famous. She appeared in vaudeville shows as a soloist, and then moved to live radio, thereby gaining fame for both herself and her instrument, which was rapidly replacing the xylophone in jazz. Mitzi Bush was possibly the most famous of the female instrumentalists appearing in vaudeville. Rated on a par with the finest male drummers, she was the featured soloist with the Parisiene Redheads, the first female band to secure a recording contract on the Brunswick label. She then toured the Keith circuit as the featured member of the Bobbie Brice all-female band, called the "Brick-Tops." Sade Ruthe Rams, a drummer with Count Bernie Vici's Symphonic Girls, was a featured attraction on both the Orpheum and Keith vaudeville circuits. Drum manufacturer William F. Ludwig recounts a meeting with Ms. Rams when she visited his factory: Mr. Ludwig subsequently gave this advice to all drummers. "Drummers, if you are not well-versed in the rudiments, talk about the weather." He stated that she was one of the best lady drummers he had ever heard.

While there were a large number of all-female bands appearing throughout the vaudeville circuits, when that era came to an end, it also marked the sudden decline of women instrumentalists. There were several all-female bands that were quite prominent during the big band era, but the number was small compared to the vast number of male bands playing throughout the country. Ina Rae Hutton led a very fine all-female band for a number of years during the era. She later changed her format and made it an all-male band. Phil Spitalny toured extensively with an excellent all-female band that also appeared in movies. The band was rated as good as most all-male bands. The Hormel Meat Packing Company formed an all-female band during the late

Marian McPartland, pianist (Courtesy: ASCAP).

forties and put it on the road performing at business meetings and corporation activities and promotional events. The band, however, was rather short-lived even though it had outstanding musicians, many of whom had just finished college, where they had concentrated on jazz studies. The singers did continue to perform and became a viable part of the all-male bands of the big band era.

Daily life was not easy. Why would women want to endure the torturous regimen of life on the road? In many cases, it meant doing a series of one-nighters across the country traveling in aging busses under horrible conditions. Being harassed both sexually and professionally by men in both the bands and the audience certainly could not have been conducive to first-rate performances. Some of the women singers that traveled with the big bands eliminated the harassment by marrying a member of the band. This posed problems when one or the other of the partners wanted to take up employment with another band. This situation would often lead to a breakup in a marriage or the retirement of one of the parties involved.

Today women are very active throughout the country in both traditional jazz and rock bands. It is still rare to find women playing along side men in previously all-male bands. There are a few women bandleaders leading male bands. Ada Cavallo is fronting the newly reorganized Latin band of Xavier Cugat, and Toshiko Akiyoshi is leading and playing piano with her all-male band. The latter is a contemporary version of pianist/composer Mary Lou Williams, who was popular during the big band and be-bop eras. An excellent, exciting, high-energy all-female band playing contemporary rock is named Miss-Behavin', and is a featured musical attraction appearing at Disneyland.

In many cases, women appear as solo performers or with a small combo in an intimate nightclub setting. Two of the finest in the professional music world are pianists Marian McPartland and Ellen Rucker. McPartland, a native of England, is the former wife of Austin High Gang trumpeter Jimmy McPartland. The two met when he was stationed in England with an army band during World War II. Following the war, she moved to the United States and has gained an enviable reputation as one of the finest jazz pianists in the country.

Maiden Voyage, Ann Patterson, director (Courtesy: David Shaner Collection).

One of the more exciting big bands in the nation is an all-female band in the Los Angeles area called Maiden Voyage, led by saxophonist Ann Patterson. While it is considered a rehearsal/kicks type band, it has made appearances as a feature on "The Tonight Show," and presents concerts in the Los Angeles area. Comprised of excellent musicians, the band generates true musical excitement when it performs. As jazz critics would state, "it swings."

However, through the eras of jazz and through the years of its development and eventual change, the prime role of women in jazz has been as vocalists. Solo song stylists such as Judy Garland, Lena Horne, Ethel Merman, Mary Martin, Barbra Streisand and current stars such as Whitney Houston, Aretha Franklin and Tina Turner did not have to endure the tortures of road travel with male bands. Credit must be given to those women who paid their dues as the big band vocalists, many of whom are still very active performers today, while others have either retired completely from music or redirected their careers and found other professions. All have made a definite contribution to the development of jazz. The great blues singers performing on the old T.O.B.A. circuit including; Bessie Smith, Mamie Smith, Ma Rainey, Ida Cox and Sippie Wallace had all retired or died prior to the big band era. The late Alberta Hunter, the last of these singers, retired and in the late seventies made a brief but rather successful comeback.

Ralph Levy, saxophonist with the Gene Krupa band when Anita O'Day was the band's vocalist, was asked what made her such a fine singer. He stated, "Anita had and still has the qualities necessary to make a tune swing. She had a great ear, a super sense of time, and the creative mind with which to improvise. This, plus a style that was unique, captivated the listener. Her vocals made the band swing ever harder. She was an asset to both the band and the era." Unfortunately, she has had her experience with drugs. Following rehabilitation, she has returned to music, and is now singing better than ever.

Professional musicians rate Ella Fitzgerald as the finest jazz singer in history. She was the vocalist with the Chick Webb orchestra and for a time, following his death, was its leader. Her improvisational skills set the standard for singers in the be-bop era. Her voice became an instrument, phrasing the riffs with the winds. She is still very active in jazz circles. Her contemporaries, Sarah Vaughn, Pearl Bailey, Keeley Smith, and Peggy Lee, continue to perform as solo singers, not affiliated with a specific band.

Others who were notable vocalists with bands were: Doris Day, Helen Forrest, Dinah Washington, Ivie Anderson, June Christy, Chris Connor, Pat

Singer Anita O'Day (Courtesy: David Shaner Collection).

Suzuki, Jackie Cain, Margaret Whiting, Paula Kelly, Kitty Kallen, Edythe Wright, Connie Haynes, Martha Tilton, Helen O'Connell, Helen Humes, Jo Stafford, Rosemary Clooney, and Billie Holiday.

Billie Holiday, also nicknamed "Lady Day" by saxophonist Lester Young, was one of the finest singers in all of jazz. A play entitled "Lady Day" currently recognizes her talent and tribulations. Her career ended much too soon because of an addiction to drugs. She was, for a brief time, the female vocalist with the Count Basie band. Unfortunately, lack of personal discipline and drug addiction was not to be tolerated by Basie. She was fired from the band and began a series of solo engagements throughout the country, including a number of record dates, the results of which have become classics in the eyes of record collectors.

The women in jazz are here to stay. They have made valuable musical contributions in all forms of jazz. The last area of participation for women has been in instrumental music. Perhaps the most significant reason

Billie Holliday (Courtesy of the Institute of Jazz Studies, Rutgers University).

for this acceptance is due to the participation of women in the school jazz programs from high school through college. Women playing in bands alongside men are developing equality.

Both men and women are studying and playing jazz in schools throughout the country today. This assures that women will be an integral part of the total jazz picture, both as vocalists and instrumentalists.

The women listed here set the stage for others of their sex to be accepted, recognized, and praised for their contributions. Well-schooled, diligent individuals, they have made very positive marks in the field of jazz.

Chapter 6
The Studio Musician

One of the choicest "gigs" in professional music is that of being on call at one of the major studios whether it is a recording studio, a movie studio, a television studio or a radio network. The work is pleasant, there is no travel involved, the hours are such that a musician can do studio work during the daytime hours and play for live audiences nights or weekends. A number of the daytime and late night talk shows employ a regular band. These shows are taped during morning or afternoon hours again allowing the musicians to undertake additional gigs during their off hours. The pay for studio work is excellent compared to club dates and casuals. The latter are not the type musicians seek because of the irregular income, forcing them to seek employment in the most demeaning fashion for a musician, a "daytime job" away from music. This can be considered a horrible fate!

The requirements for a studio musician are fundamental to the profession—promptness, dependability, no use of drugs or alcohol while on a job, outstanding musical ability and a cooperative personality. Experience in another type of studio work is also an asset.

Studio conductors are working on a strict time frame whether it be for a live show, a television series or movie background music. With those constraints, they must have the very best musicians in the business. There is little or no time for in-depth rehearsals. Musicians must be able to receive short verbal instructions, and then perform flawlessly. In studio work the adage "time is money," prevails.

Arranger/composer Sammy Nestico related an experience in which he had a recording date for a television program which required a string section consisting of first and second violins, viola, cello and string bass. One person per part had been hired. However, one of the string players was not in the studio at the appointed time. Nestico quickly rewrote the string parts eliminating the missing instrument. When the tardy musician arrived more than a half hour late, he was promptly fired and lost the opportunity for future employment with Nestico. Such an error can be very costly to a musician depending on a livelihood from studio work.

Yet, while the comfort of steady employment is an economic cushion, it does have its disadvantages. Rarely is the studio musician seen by a live audience. On talk shows, the musicians perform during commercials and are heard and seen only by the studio audience. On recordings, in movie work and for television background music, they are never seen. For some this can become a frustration. As Lloyd Ulyate relates in his interview, "There is a challenge in performing for a live audience."

Entering studio work is a difficult process. Much like the rungs of a ladder, the person with little or no experience begins at the bottom and works up to the "first call" position with a contractor, studio or conductor. Each of these people that are in a hiring position have their preferences depending on their experiences. A particular conductor may prefer certain musicians. Studios may hire musicians who have worked for them before, and contractors have lists of "preferred" people.

The contractor has the responsibility of acting as a "middle man" between the musician and the studio. It is the contractor's responsibility to determine who is best suited for a particular assignment. Of course, each has favorites and will make recommendations accordingly. The role is very important to the studios as the job is as related to excellent performances as that of the particular musician hired. Studios and conductors demand perfection from all performers regardless of the style and type of music being recorded.

The competition has become keener with the introduction of high-tech electronics to studio music. The use of synthesizers have, in some cases, completely eliminated the need for studio musicians to perform background music for movies or television. From the studio's standpoint it is a major economic move to eliminate payrolls. There is no need for recording studios, rehearsal halls, contractors, technicians, copyists, or other time and labor costing devices.

Following is an interesting insight into studio music by one of the "first call" trombonists in studio music.

Lloyd Ulyate is one of the most "in demand" trombonists on the West coast. A native of Riverside, California, he has studied and performed in the Los Angeles area most of his life. With time out for military duty as an army bandsman during World War II, and attending college as a music student, he has spent his entire career playing in radio, movie and television studios, along with performances with the big bands of Jimmy Dorsey, Al Donahue and Bobby Sherwood. He has played for a majority of movie and television composers/conductors including John Cacavas and Dave Grusin. In addition to his work in studios and with bands, he has delved into his own record company and is recording and producing his own recordings, at times playing all the tracks himself.

The author and Lloyd Ulyate became good friends while both served and performed in an army band. Playing on the same band with Lloyd was both musical training and musical satisfaction. He might as well have invented the word perfection. His orders to all who played with him were simple. Make it swing, or it's all over for you!

When asked what his most memorable studio experience has been, he quickly answers, "a record date with Louis and Ella."

Lloyd Ulyate Interview

February 13, 1988, Anaheim, California

Q: How old were you when you discovered you had a talent to become a professional musician?

Lloyd: I was probably fifteen years old and knew absolutely that I wanted to follow that course.

Q: With all your years of experience playing professionally with the big bands and in the studios, do you still practice your instrument, and if so, what routine do you follow to keep in condition?

Lloyd: I have a regular practice routine that I do every day. It takes me between forty-five minutes and an hour-and-a-half, depending on how much I rest in between. My routine requires me to play and rest and play and rest.

Q: On the West coast, which is a sort of hub for professional musicians, if a young person wanted to become a part of the music here, where would you advise him to go to learn to be a professional player?

Lloyd: That's a good question. If I were a young player and wanted to concentrate on playing jazz, I don't think there are any teachers here who could be of any help. If I wanted to work in the studios, as competitive as the business is now, I would probably go to the Eastman School of Music, or I would go to any great conservatory that has a good teacher for my particular instrument and study it from a ''legit'' approach.

Q: As a musical foundation?

Lloyd: Absolutely, because the way the music business is set up now, what's left of the studio business has changed so much because of the synthesizer, used on the kind of programs that are on television now. There used to be a large number of variety shows and music shows. Well, there are none of those now. Our studio work is essentially motion pictures and television, which is basically ''legit'' playing.

Q: Do you consider yourself primarily a studio musician?

Lloyd: Absolutely. I still enjoy going out and doing a live performance in front of an audience. I enjoy the challenge. I believe it's much harder to play a live performance than it is to play in a studio.

Q: When you got out of the army after World War II, did you return to college to prepare yourself for a studio career?

Lloyd: No, I didn't. I wanted to return to school, but a strange set of events took place in which you and the rest of your army band were involved. If you recall, you were all being transferred to Fort Sam Houston in Texas. Well, while you were on that train going to Texas, I had been discharged and was heading back home to California. Anyway, on your same train was the Al Donahue band. You guys got into a conversation with them and mentioned the fact that I had just been discharged and was heading home. I had not been home one day when he called and asked if I would like to come on the band immediately. He said, ''We're going on a trip to the Northwest for three weeks.'' I said, ''Fine!'' and I went right back to work. It was the only time Donahue went on the road with the band.

Q: Was it a good band?

Lloyd: Yes. Stan Getz played on the band. He was the most famous member.

Q: Did you play with the big bands while breaking into studio work?

Lloyd: I started to play with some of the local bands, and then I got a call to join Charlie Barnett's band. I also worked with Ike Carpenter's band and Bobby Sherwood. All the big bands seemed to be here and I would get calls from all of them. There used to be a magazine that Capitol Records put out. When I was with Al's band, they wrote a big article about me playing with his band—''Young Kid Sparks Band.'' Evidently that did me a lot of good.

Q: When did you join Jimmy Dorsey's band?

Lloyd: About 1947. He and his brother, Tommy, owned this ballroom in Ocean Park called the Casino Gardens. Jimmy's band would play there three nights a week, and the rest of the time was spent in the studios making band shows and a couple of feature films.

Q: Doing studio playing and playing with big bands for live audiences is like wearing two hats. Of the two, rumor has it that studio work is the most demanding and that immediate perfection is required, with little or no rehearsal time. Is this the case?

Lloyd: I believe the first requisite is to be able to play your instrument well. You must be able to follow the conductor, to be adaptable to all styles of music, be a pretty good citizen and don't goof up.

Q: You're saying be dependable?

Lloyd: Someone asked Barney Castle what was the first prerequisite in working for the studios, and he said, "Find a place to park your car." No, I think it's always striving for perfection. This may sound simplistic, but it's really true. Ninety percent of the music is very simple. My brother, Bill, who's a saxophone player at Twentieth Century Fox, says, "Studio business is ninety-five percent boring and five percent terror." But what I'm trying to say is that basically, it's very simple music, most of the time. So, what you have to do is learn how to play simple music extremely well.

Q: That sounds like learning the fundamentals of music.

Lloyd: Absolutely. Many people, and I'm not mentioning any names, famous people (and I'm not putting them down, because I have such admiration for them and what they do), are not really fitted for studio work. The studios want you to play whole notes in tune and with a nice sound. And they want sixteenth notes that are sixteenth notes and eighth notes that are eighth notes.

Q: We have come to believe that studio work is the toughest. You have to be able to read the ink right off the page.

Lloyd: Yes, we have those moments, and we have to do just that. Much of the music is very difficult, but most of it is really very simple. You have to have the ability to possess a great fundamental knowledge of music and command of your instrument and be able to play simple music very well.

Q: How much importance do you place on the rapport between the leader or conductor and the player?

Lloyd: A lot. When you're a commercial player and a man hires you, then it's your duty to please him. You're only going to be there for three hours, so if you don't like the guy, or if you don't like the music, that's immaterial. He's hired you, so you're going to do the best that you can for him. If he says, "Hey, I don't like the way you're playing it. Do it a different way," you say, "Sure." No matter what the music is; good, bad, terrible, if you're going to be a commercial musician, you're going to do what he says. And certainly, if you're a band leader, you don't want a bunch of guys in your band who don't like you and won't do what you say. You're not going to use them anymore, are you?

Q: What have your years in the studios been like?

Lloyd: Around 1948, I began working in radio, and then in the movie studios. My big band experience only lasted a couple years, except we played big band music in the studios. Time-Life did a series where we recreated eleven of the big bands. We spent two years working on that project, doing one or two dates a week. There are about twelve or thirteen of these albums out. Billy May took all the arrangements off the original records, and so we recreated practically every big band there was. I was very fortunate to be a part of that project.

Q: You've ventured into recording in recent years. How much of that do you do, and what are you doing with it?

Lloyd: Oh, I haven't gone into it in a big way. I've been experimenting with an eight-track recorder and a mixer. I have an old RCA 44B ribbon mike, which is still the best microphone for brass instruments. It came out in 1932 and is still the best. That's not just my opinion. We use these microphones in the studios to get the brass instruments.

Q: Now, what do you do with the recordings?

Lloyd: I'm experimenting with them. I'm making tracks to play with. I may make another album, if it comes out pretty good.

Q: What do you do with the albums, once you've produced them?

Lloyd: I sell them to trombone players, or just give them away. You know a trombone album is a very limited market. I have a DX-7 synthesizer, an Apple computer, and several programs for sequencing music, along with an echo machine and a nice board. It all makes for interesting experimentation. Some of the things on the DX-7 sound pretty good, like some of the harp sounds, and the bass sound.

Q: So you could put the sound of a whole orchestra behind you?

Lloyd: Well, not really. It's not going to sound like an orchestra. You can't make a synthesizer sound like an orchestra, but you can make it sound like good music, if you approach it from the standpoint that, "I'm not going to try to duplicate an orchestra. I'm going to make a new sound."

Q: So, if you wanted to, could you be working six or seven days a week, year 'round?

Lloyd: Not now. At one time that was possible.

Q: Is there just not that much opportunity today?

Lloyd: The music business has changed a great deal in recent years. The advent of the synthesizer and synthesized music has really hurt the commercial field. They've taken over, especially brass instruments. For example, on television, the kinds of shows that we did were usually cops and robbers, detective shows, spy pictures, anything that had any kind of excitement to it. They used a lot of brass instruments. Now, all of these shows have been taken over by the synthesizer. "Miami Vice," for example, was a terrible thing for the musicians, because it was the first show that really used the synthesizer. So, if you're a producer and say, "I want to have a show like 'Miami Vice,'" it will have synthesized music. Also, in the old days, there was a great deal of live television, big variety shows. I can remember when there must have been twelve variety shows originating in Los Angeles. I did the Red Skelton show for twenty-one years. It was a great job. I worked on all kinds of them, Glen Campbell, Carol Burnett. That's all gone now. We used to do one or two specials a month. Now you don't see any musical specials. We also did lots of recordings. Most of that's gone, too, because many records are now made in someone's garage. We used to do a large number of jingles/commercials, but most of them are done by synthesizer today. So, the only thing that's really left that's viable is movies. Fortunately, there are a lot of movies being made. And, movies are doing better than ever, because there are so many ways a man (producer) can get his money back, besides showing it in a theater. He can go to cassettes, he can go to cable, and he can go to television. He can also go to foreign release. So, what's left for the studio musicians in Los Angeles is movies. They are the best we have.

Q: Besides your music, what personal things have you done and do you enjoy doing?

Lloyd: I love to ski. I love to play golf. I love my children, and I love to travel. I have a very good life.

Q: In the years you have left as a studio musician, what goals and achievements have you set for yourself before you retire?

Lloyd: I don't think I'm ever going to hang it up. I'm never going to stop playing. And as far as studio work is concerned, I'll play in them until they don't call me anymore.

Lloyd Ulyate Recordings:

Time-Life Series—The Swinging Years
John Williams—ET, Close Encounters
Lloyd Ulyate & His Trombone
Porgy & Bess—Louie Armstrong & Ella

Chapter 7

Movie and Television Music

Since the advent of the talking picture music has been an integral part of the action on the screen. Movie music replaced the pit orchestra or small ensemble which played music that was sent to the movie theaters along with the film. Occasionally, the house pianist was given the option to improvise appropriate music to coincide with the action on the screen. The music was to enhance the plot and dialogue when talking pictures became well-established. Love scenes required music that was tranquil and melodious but would not detract from the action or dialogue. The tempo was moderate to slow, giving viewers a relaxed and comfortable feeling. Scenes with fast-paced action including fights, automobile racing and crashes, and the ever-popular western complete with range war or Indian war, required music with faster tempos, played by the brass and percussion with explosive sound effects thrown in.

A very small but elite group of musicians became the composers and conductors for the movie industry. The music involves a complicated form of composition, much of it written by a mathmatical formula that is required when the music has definite time constraints. Composer/arranger Sammy Nestico, in presenting a lecture-demonstration at a music conference, described the problems facing the composer. He indicated the necessity of coordination between film and music in a hypothetical situation. Scene: Car goes over cliff and will crash in rocks at seashore and explode. Music must be timed perfectly so when the car impacts on rocks, a heavy chord is played by the orchestra. If the chord is played prior to impact, scene is destroyed. If the chord is sounded after impact, scene is likewise destroyed. Everything must be synchronized so the impact appears and the music is heard at exactly the same moment. It is often the suggestions of the director and producer that determine the type and style of music to be used for specific scenes, as well as for the whole production. Background music for ''Keystone Kops'' movies included much humor and a number of sound effects giving the whole scene a good deal of hilarity, whereas movies that indicate tragedy, war, religion, or serious, social-economic crisis will require music of a very serious heavy nature.

Composers such as Frank Skinner, Vladimer Bakalinikov, Max Steiner and John Cacavas were early masters at composing music for films. They were later joined by men such as Andre Previn and Henry Mancini, who put jazz effects into the movie scores. Today, Quincy Jones and Dave Grusin are the leaders in the field. Jazz-oriented, they have found a new freedom in writing for movies. No longer must they adhere to the restrictions that forced earlier composers to match the mood of the music with that of the scene. Actual recordings of some of the rock bands are permissible. Using excerpts of classical music with a contemporary instrumentation and rhythmic treatment is also quite acceptable. The opening scene of the movie ''Bob and Carol, Ted and Alice'' is accompanied by a rock band playing the ''Hallelujah Chorus'' from Handel's *Messiah.''*

Movie and television composers have a tendency to favor composing for movies over television. Movies are produced in a time frame that includes an open end for completion. This gives the composer flexibility in his work. Television, particularly a weekly series, has no open end. Everything has a definite deadline for completion. As composer Dave Grusin indicates in the following interview, with television composing, you have time for nothing else. The television show and the impending deadlines rule your entire life.

Perhaps the tight scheduling for composing was partly responsible for the use of synthesizers in movie and TV music. The composer, working with a synthesizer, could produce the sounds of a band or orchestra with the machine. This was faster than waiting until the film was complete, then hiring and rehearsing the orchestra, and working with the film in the studio. The major complaint of studio musicians in recent years has been that they are being replaced by the synthesizer. The musicians are convinced that the sounds produced by synthesizers do not compare with those of the actual instrument being performed. Studios, on the other hand, feel that movie and television audiences are not so perceptive that machine-produced music will distract them from enjoying the film.

A compliment to the movie composers is the inclusion of a category in the annual Academy Awards presentation for film music. It recognizes the importance that music has in a film.

Following is an interview with one of Hollywood's leading composers. Throughout the interview, readers will get an intimate look into the making of movie music. It should also give one an appreciation of music as an integral part of a movie.

Dave Grusin is a native of Denver Colorado. He received his formal training at the University of Colorado, and maintains ties with the University's music program, serving on the music school's advisory board. A proponent of electronic music, he is aware of the impact of electronics on all forms of music, from live performances to music for movies and television. As a performer, he has played piano for the Benny Goodman band in 1960 and with Quincy Jones from 1971 to 1973. He is a consultant for the Yamaha instrument manufacturing company, and, along with a partner, has formed GRP, a recording company. They have produced a number of albums under that label. He received an Academy Award nomination for his musical score for the movie, "On Golden Pond," and has just completed the score for the Robert Redford production, "The Milagro Beanfield War." In addition, he is given credit for the theme of the successful television series, "St. Elsewhere." The father of three children, he makes his home in Santa Fe, New Mexico.

Dave Grusin Interview

April 14, 1988, Boulder, Colorado

Q: What percentage of your scoring for movie and television is done by high tech as opposed to the traditional method of scoring for full orchestra?

Dave: I'm doing some scoring by synthesizer. The percentage, I guess would be a third electronically, two-thirds acoustically. The last film I did, "The Milagro Beanfield War," was done acoustically. I don't do that much television. The last thing that I did was "St. Elsewhere," which was about four or five years ago. That was all electronic. I think the nature of the project is going to determine how it's done. Certainly it has a lot to do with the size of orchestras and what kind of orchestra.

Q: Describe your "home" studio where you do your writing. What type equipment are you presently using in your writing/scoring?

Dave: My little home studio consists of a couple of synthesizers, Yamaha DX-7's, some effects, a small mixing board, a cassette player to record with, and a computer to actually make digital recordings of tracks. I have a computer called an Atari ST, and a software program for that called Hybrid Arts Midi-Track. This software is in the nature of a sixty-track recording studio, so that I can play a part on it and then play a part on another track, and then continue to over-dub. If I had enormous numbers of instruments, I guess theoretically I could put on up to sixty tracks, and they'd all be of different instruments. But, it does help to make demos of film scores, particularly. They're not the final product, but as I'm writing, it helps if I can record something in terms of the theme with a patch on the synthesizer that sounds vaguely like the ultimate acoustic instrumentation that it's going to be—in the case of the Milagro picture for Redford, there was a theme played on guitar with strings. I had both of those sounds available to me on the synthesizer, so I made a demo for myself to see if the theme would work with the picture, as well as to play for the director. And to play it that way for him, on a cassette, so that he can hear not the final product, but some kind of demonstration of what the final sound is going to be, it's pretty valuable for both of us. That's my little home outfit. When a project is finished, I just turn in a score, and in that case (Milagro), we then hired an orchestra. The demo was purely for our own "work in progress" use, so we could hear it as we went along.

Q: When you contract with a studio for a film or television program, how large a staff of assistants are you allowed and what are their roles?

Dave: I don't use orchestrators, normally, but if I did, I suppose they would be part of the assistants. I do use copyists, and the studio pays for them. They also pay for a music editor. The only time this wouldn't be true is if I took a package, I think. If I said, "You give me X amount of dollars, and I'll deliver the score to you, and I'll be responsible for writing it, recording it, having it copied, and having it edited to work with your film." I've never done that.

Q: Do you have any say in who the conductor will be?

Dave: I'm usually the conductor. I'm usually hired to do that, as well as to be responsible for the band. There's another person involved called a contractor, who is necessary to call an orchestra. Sometimes he is from the studio but not necessarily. Sometimes I use an outside contractor. He goes on the payroll as a sideman, right on the contract, as far as the union is concerned. The music editor first takes the film and times the musical sequence, so you know exactly how long the cues are, where they start, where they stop, and what the internal things are that happen. Then, after the recording and mixing, the editor will actually take the music that has been mixed, and cut that so that it is in sync with the picture. That's the function of the music editor. The editor usually has an assistant, because that's a lot of work.

Q: Describe the changes in film composing and scoring that have taken place during this past decade.

Dave: The primary change is the development of technology, since music is now made not only acoustically, but digitally as well. There's been a use of that technology in some areas to try to save money—to save salaries. Rather than hire twenty-four strings, you put it on a couple of tracks with a synthesizer. Generally, that doesn't work so well. The best use of synthetic music is to do things that you can't do acoustically. That's the exciting use of that stuff, not to try to fool anybody or to replace existing sounds. That would be the biggest single factor. Another factor is that films have changed a lot in the last ten years. The majority of films coming out of Hollywood are clinically and scientifically directed at an audience, and I don't know what the age is, but I'd guess it would be between fifteen and twenty-four or so. There's a whole science now about who's going to see this picture, how many people can we expect to see it, and that will determine how much we're going to spend on making it. If you make a film for a certain demographic age group in that area, a logical choice of music for that picture would be music which that age group listens to. So that's why we see a lot of songs in pictures now, by hit name groups, Phil Collins and U2 and David Byrne and Talking

Heads, and so forth. The film maker is using the ancillary contemporary media of music, to use in his contemporary film.

Q: What are the procedures for adapting music to film?

Dave: It's basically mathematics. Three feet of thirty-five millimeter film go by every two seconds. So if I have a scene in a picture that's sixty feet long that needs music, I have to know that the cue is going to be forty seconds long, so there's a three to two ratio. Now, what that means is, if the cue starts at zero and runs for forty seconds, we'll be at the sixty foot increment of film. The way it specifically works, I don't think about footage at all. I think about time—seconds. So my tempo might be four seconds per bar. That means I've got ten bars in forty seconds. So, you see, it does finally come down to be mathematical formulas. Now, the way I determine that my tempo is four seconds per bar is another matter. It's best that I determine the tempo first, and then measure it, and then I can find out where I'm going to be. The tempo can correlate directly with the action on the screen. You have the option of doing that. In the old way of scoring films, they tried to do that, absoluely. They tried to match action with tempo. A newer way to do it is to try not to do that; to try to do some kind of counterpart to the tempo of the film and speed of the action, and not hit every cue. You know, when the guy closes the door, try not to have the big chord hit on the door anymore. That used to be almost the gospel. Click tracks are a device to keep everybody on tempo. If I've got something going four seconds to a bar and I hear a click on each beat, I'll hear it on each second, and therefore I'll know I'll be absolutely right on the tempo at the end of that forty second cue.

Q: What musical processes change when composing music for live public performances versus composing for the screen?

Dave: The nature of live music is that the music is the medium. The nature of film is that film is the medium, and it's absolutely the boss, so that you can't ever forget that you're serving this film. That's not to say you can't be musical in the process, but live music certainly is an entity of its own. That is the end, and in the other case, it's the means.

Q: What specific skills do you feel you possess that allowed you to enter the professional arena of Hollywood composers/arrangers?

Dave: When I first started to do this, I had an agent who had ninety-five composers on his roster, and he had them listed in terms of who was on top, and then the next guys down. I used to get jobs, I think, when the first guys were not available. Then they'd come to my name and he'd sell me. Then I'd have to find out who they'd called for, that they really wanted, so I'd know who I was supposed to be when I got there. And I'm talking about people like Mancini, and Burt Bacharach and Elmer Bernstein, and so forth. I tried to be somewhat eclectic. I tried to incorporate any style I could to do the film. My whole sense of my beginnings in this was a workshop nature. In retrospect, the whole thing was a workshop. Every film demanded different things. One of the things I could do was be somewhat of a chameleon and adapt to whatever a film needed.

Q: You still have opportunities to play live performances and produce recordings. What type of group and what specific instrumentation do you use?

Dave: We make recordings, but I don't have any specific size group that I am locked into in terms of recordings. My brother, Don, and I just finished recording, just the two of us, all electronic. He's a keyboard player, as well, and we did the whole thing with the computer that I mentioned before. We programmed it and played to it and played live with it, and so forth, and made the record so that nobody else was on the record except the two of us. That's one way to do it. On the one before that, I used the London Symphony Orchestra, for the Cinemagic album last year. So there's no set rule in terms of what I'm doing. I don't do much live performing. I sometimes play with a guy who does, one of the artists on our label, named Lee Ritenour. I'll go out and do concerts with him. In fact, we just got back from one in Europe with Lee and Tom Scott and a rhythm section. We did some one-nighters, but that's not my life as a rule.

Q: Looking to the future, what academic/musical preparation do you feel will be required for professional composers/arrangers in the twenty-first century?

Dave: I like that question, but I don't know how to answer it. I just talked to a kid who said, "Don't you think computers are going to ruin music? It's not going to be as sensitive as it once was, and shouldn't somebody be practicing their instrument instead of playing with their computer?" And I said, "Well, if you are a viola player, you better practice the viola and leave the computer alone. If you're going to be in electronic music, the computer is your instrument, so you'd better practice that." I think that the preparation in that area has to be addressed academically. I'm quite interested in this college (University of Colorado). I'm on faculty board, and one of the things that I'm interested in seeing is intensifying whatever the electronic opportunities are. I'm not saying everybody should do it, but if a keyboard major wants to have a career later on, either as a composer/arranger or as a player in the studios, he should somehow get himself a good, solid electronic keyboard education. It's not easy to do that all at the same time. I'm still learning my computer. My children all grew up in the computer era, but it's really hard for me. I have to do it a step at a time. By the time I get one instrument figured out, it's obsolete. The state of the art changes every six months. With this stuff it's a constant learning process, and I think it would be great to formalize that a little bit academically. It is sometimes looked down on as the "stepchild" of music education, but for somebody who's going to be a player and actually make a living playing music in the future, he's going to have to know something about that, unless he's an acoustic virtuoso and only going to deal with symphony orchestras.

Q: What composers/arrangers do you enjoy listening to for your personal enjoyment?

Dave: I don't listen to much music, but when I do, I listen to classical music. I listen to Stravinsky. Stravinsky is maybe my all-time guy, if I had to pick one favorite composer, certainly of the twentieth century composers. Bach is always fascinating to me—the French composers like Poulanc, Milhaud, Debussy and Ravel. Brahms is something I get into. I don't listen to much jazz. I don't listen to much current stuff, except as it relates to our record company and my work.

Q: When you first entered the field of composition, who were the people that became your inspiration?

Dave: Nobody in particular. I thought when I was here at the university, in the early fifties, that maybe film music was some kind of frontier that I could look at in some kind of pragmatic way. Not too many American composers are making a living composing. So I thought about that. One man in particular stood out at the time, and that was Andre Previn, who was then head of the music department at MGM. He was this "wunder kind" from Berlin. I think he came to this country when he was eight years old. He was a marvelous pianist—a serious pianist and also a very good jazz pianist. I thought he was a great film composer. He didn't do that many films. He opted to bail out on that and do what he's doing now, which is dealing only with classical music, conducting. I have a lot of idols in that field, but I remember him specifically from those years, as being influential to me. He was one of the first modernists, changing the nature of scoring from the old Max Steiner school, and putting in these new elements, these modern, jazzy elements. (At that time I thought anything having to do with jazz was going to save the music world.) I picked up on that. Mancini was a master at it. The more one does it, the more one sees how hard it is to do, and the less pleased one is with the results. It's not easy. Quincy Jones is another one who did that same sort of jazz-oriented type of scoring, even more than I did. I've kind of drifted away from the straight jazz element, and I'll do a picture that has none of that in it now. I guess I've become more interested in serious writing and less interested in film writing, over a period of time, although it's been a wonderful profession, and the need for it continues.

Q: You are in the profession of music, but in that field you are divided between two major facets, that of a performer and that of a composer. How are you able to handle both areas so well?

Dave: I really don't spend much time on the performance part of my career. I do spend time with the record company, in production, and administration. Luckily, I have a partner who's a crazy workaholic that runs the company. It's grown so much now that there are thirty people working at GRP Records in New York. I moved from there a little over a year ago. I just couldn't live in New York anymore, so I've moved to New Mexico, and it means that I do a lot of commuting, but it's still better than living in the middle of that city.

Q: One of your best known movie scores is for the film "On Golden Pond." How long did it take you to complete the score, and how were you involved in the actual recording of the music?

Dave: This was nominated for an Academy Award, but besides the nomination, the thing I remember most about "Golden Pond" is the fact that the film was a special film for music, because it had a lot of space in it, and a lot of need for a certain kind of ambience in the music. This is very rare. I have never worked on another film that had that kind of opportunity. The score has a lot of space in it as well, and usually there's not time in each segment of music to take that kind of time. It was a pleasure to work on. I don't know that that's my favorite picture, but in terms of my working experience, it's probably my best one, the one that I had the most fun with and that was the most satisfying. I must have spent six weeks on the picture. Prior to that I had gone to location and had a couple of talks with the director. I think we recorded it over a period of three days. The first day, I just did the piano part. I went in with the picture and had the picture streamered and marked and organized, and played only the piano part to the picture. Then the second two days we brought the orchestra in, and we played on other tracks to those same cues. It was great. One of the best parts of the experience was that the director loved everything from the beginning, and continued to love it until the film was released, which is rare. I met the Fondas on location. Jane actually had control over the music, because her company was the producer of the film, but she didn't surface in that phase of the film at all.

Q: On the television series, "St. Elsewhere," you are credited with the musical theme for the show. Are you also responsible for any of the music for the continuing weekly segments?

Dave: I only did the first show, and the theme. A fellow named J.A.C. Redford, to my knowledge, did all of the segments of the show, a really talented kid who's now blossoming and doing a lot of nice projects. I loved what he did, because he took the kind of generic quality of the titles of the theme and we extracted the first cues. He used that for over four years. We talk occasionally, and it's a very nice experience for me to have somebody dealing with my material in that way, in a way that I would have loved to do it myself.

Q: What is the difference in writing for a movie and writing for a television series? Do either have specific restrictions for a composer?

Dave: Mostly, it's in terms of time. Television is a voracious medium that leaves no time for anything. With film, at least you have a little breathing room. Most of the time you have six weeks. You're supposed to have ten weeks, but I don't think I ever have had that much time. But in television, if you're doing a series, and it's a show that's on every week, that's what your life is, because you only have the film long enough to barely get it done and get it copied and performed.

Q: How did you become involved with composing/scoring for movies and television?

Dave: I became involved with film television and movies through live television. I was working for a singer named Andy Williams. I had a band and was music director for a show he did in the early sixties at NBC. It was a television variety show. The producer of that show branched out and had a couple of other film shows going at Screen Gems. He asked me if I'd be interested in doing them. It was an opportunity to get into the film medium. I also did some bad sit-coms for a couple of years, but as I said before, my whole life has been a workshop, so I don't think anything is ever lost. There's never anything wasted there.

Q: Are you on any particular schedule of composing and if so, how many projects are you involved in during the same time period?

Dave: In composing, I try to do one thing at a time. Otherwise I find it hard for my own sense of concentration. If I'm desperately trying to come up with a theme for one project, the idea of trying to come up with a theme for something else is horrendous. I try not to do that. A couple of times I've had to double up, but never on purpose. Sometimes I'll be on a picture that will go overtime. They'll make changes and I'll need to do some additional work, and I will have already started a new project, so I'll have to go back and do a little bit of double duty. I don't mind doing that, but the idea of trying to create two things at once is tough.

Q: On your personal goals, do you plan to continue both facets (composing/performing) indefinitely, and if not, which will you give up to continue the other?

Dave: I'm sure I would give up performing. I don't know that I would ever give up composing. If you write music, that's what you do and almost who you are.

Q: How do you spend your leisure time? Do you have any favorite hobbies or activities? Are you involved in anything outside of music?

Dave: I'm involved with alot of things. I love sports, specifically skiing and tennis. And, having grown up in Colorado, just getting back in the mountains is great. Probably my favorite sport is fly fishing. If I could ever figure out a way to make a living fly fishing, I would be doing that. I just think it's the best thing.

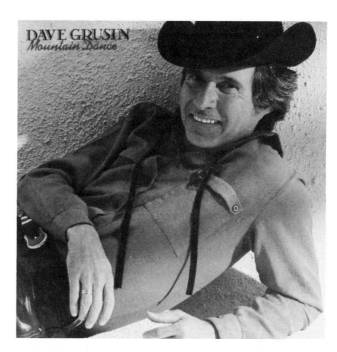

Dave Grusin album

Recordings by Dave Grusin:

Subways are for Sleeping (Epic)
Piano, Strings & Moonlight (Columbia)
Kaleidoscope (Columbia)
Discovered Again (Sheffield)
One of a Kind (GRP)
Mountain Dance (GRP)
Out of the Shadows (GRP)
NY/LA Dream Band (GRP)
Nightliner (GRP)
Harlequin (GRP)
Cinemagic (GRP)
Sticks & Stones (GRP)

Chapter 8
The Record Industry

It has been said that the recording industry makes the decision as to who will become successful in the field of popular music. The industry has the power to determine whom it will promote and whom it will ignore. While this is a rather ambiguous statement, there must be some credence given to it. Without recordings, a performer has no hope of achieving any fame whatsoever. On the other hand, many would-be stars are not of the caliber necessary to be supported by the record-buying public.

The A & R men in the recording industry are responsible for making the decisions concerning who is a worthwhile investment for all the time and effort spent in recording, promoting and marketing an individual or group. Artist & Repertoire people are specialists in determining what will or will not sell to the public. Errors on their part can prove to be a costly liability to a record company. On the other hand, a musical discovery such as the young Elvis Presley proved to be one of the biggest windfalls a record company could have.

It is rumored that the race recordings Bessie Smith made for a record company that was subsidiary of Columbia Records, which were sold in the black communities, helped keep Columbia solvent through the weak economic years. Her recordings have now been re-recorded and released as LP's under the Columbia label.

The actual recording is merely the beginning of a complicated process during which large numbers of people become intricately involved. Marketing is perhaps the most important single factor in the making of a star in popular music. Promoters spend a good deal of time urging airplay by stations throughout the country. Once this is accomplished, follow-up with personal appearances nationwide must take place. Record shops must have promotional materials, as well as ample supplies of records, to make sales worthwhile. Making the Top 40 list and maintaining a place on it week after week is a must for the record and in turn for the artist(s) to be successful. Only then will the record company begin to recoup any part of its investment.

Chet Atkins, having spent most of his career as a guitarist, became the A & R man for RCA. He later became its vice-president, a position he held for a number of years.

He is one of the founders of the country music movement. He had his beginnings during a time when the general public referred to his music as "hillbilly" music because of its geographic origin. Having the distinction of being hired and fired by some of the very finest people in country music, he nevertheless was a driving force in its development. In the opening statement of his biography, *Country Gentleman*, he states the following about his early years: "We were so poor and everybody around us was so poor that it was the forties before anyone knew there had been a depression."

From those very meager beginnings and limited early musical training, he has become one of the premier guitarists in the country. Having retired from RCA and now doing recordings with CBS Records, he continues to maintain an active performing and recording schedule. His recent work on Garrison Keillhor's "Prairie Home Companion" television show has thrust him into the national spotlight, where his guitar playing is a highlight of every show.

Of the many recording stars he has discovered, his most famous find was the young, unknown, Elvis Presley. He was also instrumental in helping the career of singer Eddy Arnold.

While often inaccurately stereotyped as a country guitarist, he has performed with Arthur Fielder and the Boston "Pops" Orchestra, and was a big winner at the Newport Jazz Festival.

He resides in Nashville, Tennessee, where he has formed his own company called CGP (Certified Guitar Player) Productions, and from this office he manages a very active career. He is a very humble, unassuming individual, with one of the most likeable personalities in the entire music industry. His interview gives the reader a close look at someone who has been on both sides of the recording industry fence.

Chet Atkins Interview

March 22, 1988, Nashville, Tennessee

Q: You are widely recognized as Mr. Guitar among your peers and the public. How old were you when you began playing the guitar? What made you select this particular instrument and who were your influences?

Chet: I started playing guitar when I was six or eight, I guess. I played ukulele before the guitar, and when a string would break, I would rip a string off an old screen door that the dog had run through, and tune that up. I told the story years ago, and people pick up on it all the time, but it's really true. I selected the guitar, I suppose, because my older brother played it. My dad played some and taught guitar. It was kind of a romantic instrument to me. I just loved the looks and the sound of it. We had other instruments around, but the guitar really appealed to me.

Q: With whom did you study the instrument?

Chet: I'm self-taught. I watched my dad teach people to play, but I already knew more about the instrument than he, so I didn't learn much from him. But anyway, with me it was kind of

Chet Atkins (Courtesy of Melodie Gimple).

"monkey see, monkey do." I stole everything I would see somebody else do that I could use in my repertoire of licks. I listened to a lot of records. I listened to piano, saxophone, and all kinds of instruments at a radio station where I worked. I listened to a lot of great guitarists, and just learned that way, and learned to read music on my own.

Q: When, where, and what were the circumstances of your entering the world of professional music?

Chet: Of course, I always wanted to get in the music business. I never dreamed that I would excel at it, but I hoped that I would be able to play on a radio station somewhere. That was the way to be heard back in those days, when I was a kid. There was a Baptist preacher who had a radio show in Columbus, Georgia, and he heard me pickin' and singin' one day and invited me to perform on his radio show, and that was the first really professional-type work I ever did on radio. When the war started, I went to Knoxville and hung around awhile. Eventually I heard that a couple of guys needed a fiddle player, so I got a job playing fiddle with those two guys, Bill Carlisle and Archie Campbell. A few days later, the boss of the radio station, Lowell Blanchard heard me playing guitar, and he gave me a spot on the show each day playing a guitar solo. It was kind of a problem, because I only knew about three tunes, and so he pressured me a lot to learn new music and learn new songs.

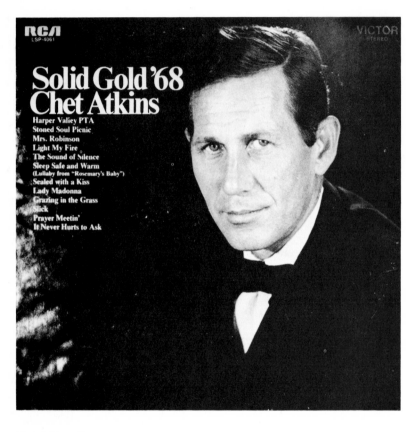

Chet Atkins album

Q: You have performed with the world's finest musicians. Which ones stand out the most in your memory, and what is there about them that so classifies them with you?

Chet: Oh, I've performed with a lot of great musicians, yes, everybody, you know, from the Boston Pops to jazz artists like George Benson and Johnny Smith, the great jazz player. They all stand out in my mind. They're not people I want to copy, or anything like that, but I admire so much their abilities on their particular instruments. George Benson, for instance, has the greatest coordinated hands I think I've ever seen, and Johnny Smith is just a terrific musician and arranger. I've always admired him.

Q: As a person who had a major influence on the development of the modern electric guitar, what do you see as potential future developments?

Chet: I don't see much change in the electric guitar in the future. I see different body styles and all that, but you know, you put a pick-up in under a string, a magnetic pick-up, and you get sound. We're experimenting at Gibson with a piezo electric pick-up which we have on a guitar that they market under my name, which gets a little different sound. And you can get into synthesizers and all that, but when the synthesizer is predominant, then that is not a guitar anymore, it's more like a keyboard instrument. I don't see much change in guitars, but I do see people becoming more and more efficient and adept at playing them, and I think players will just become more and more astonishing. That's been my experience throughout my life. I think there are more great players around now than ever.

Q: In recent years, you have become associated with the recording industry. What is your position in this industry and to what extent are you involved?

Chet: I was an artist and repertoire man with a record company for years. That's RCA, of course. I don't do that anymore. I don't have a position with a record company anymore. I just make my own records, and I tour a little bit, and play my guitar and play a little golf. Once in a while I'll produce an album with someone.

I've produced an album recently with Garrison Keillhor, and produced one two or three years ago with Roger Whittaker, and may do another one with Roger this year. But that's not really hard work, because they come in with the tunes that they want to do, and so I don't have to spend a lot of time searching for material. But that's about the extent of my involvement. Maybe I'll produce one album every two years.

Q: From your perspective as an executive in the recording industry, what, in your opinion, shapes public taste in music? Does the public demand a certain kind of music, or does the industry shape public taste?

Chet: There is a lot of conformity in radio stations and promoters which affects the taste of the public. I think America is in bad shape as far as the music business is concerned, because the play list is so small at the majority of the radio stations. People are not exposed to all kinds of music, and I think that's a shame. I know when I go to England, I hear all kinds of music and music from all the different eras, and it's sure a lot more entertaining when radio is like that. I don't think they pay a lot of attention over there to the charts of the trade magazines, and it makes for a lot nicer musical atmosphere.

Q: You were involved in the rapid rise in popularity of the late Elvis Presley. Was Elvis truly a trend-setter, or was he a catalyst for what was to be an inevitable development for that time?

Chet: Yes, I was involved with Elvis. I hired the band when he first recorded here, and the singers and everything, and played rhythm guitar. Yeah, Elvis--was he a trend-setter? Of course he was. He was the greatest trend-setter I have ever known. I've never seen anyone who had such an impact on the music business. And it was because he was so very, very different from anyone else in the world. I don't ever expect to see another one in my lifetime like Elvis.

Q: As an artist and a musician with a high degree of sensitivity, how were you able to strike a balance between commercial demands and your own desires for personal expression?

Chet: I'm very lucky, because I'm kind of square. I like melody played in various ways, and what I really like, the public usually likes, too. I'm so lucky in that respect. It would be terrible if I were a way-out jazz musician and my taste were so far away from the public. I think it's very hard to make a living when you're in that situation.

Q: The recording industry is quite complex. What procedures are involved in signing a performer, getting him or her recorded, and successfully marketing the finished product?

Chet: The procedure I used back eight or ten years ago was this. I'd just sign an artist to a recording contract and look around for some great songs. Listen to one hundred to find one good one. That's the reason it's so much work. I'd go in to the studio and try to make a great record, and then hope that we could get it started in some city somewhere in the United States. And usually, if we could get it started in one city, we could spread it all over the country. I don't think it's that easy anymore.

Q: In early jazz, the songplugger played an important role in promoting the composers and performers. In the recording industry today, how is this handled, and by whom?

Chet: I really don't know about marketing and promotion. Most of the record companies now hire outside promoters to plug their songs with radio stations. That's where it is right now. Get someone to play the record on the air. So the story today is to get the record played on the radio. Of course, the problem is that radio only has twenty or thirty slots of records to play, and to put your record on, they've got to kick one off. So, it's not all that easy. It invites a lot of payola and graft and corruption that is terrible for the business. They clean it up every few years and then it gets bad again. A lot of things are being conducted in the wrong manner, but I suppose not much can be done.

Q: Who are some of the artists that you have been influential in signing to recording contracts with RCA, and what is there about them that convinces you that they have the potential to become recording stars?

Chet: I was associated with a lot of artists--pop artists, country artists; people like Perry Como and Al Hirt. I made all of Hirt's hits, along with a lot of country stars, like Jim Reeves and Don Gibson. It's been fun. I think the person that excels in any business is the person with the most ambition and the person who tries the hardest. That's been my experience in handling artists. The person with the most talent a lot of times doesn't make it, because he may be a little lazy, but if a person is smart and works within his limitations, and tries very, very hard, sometimes he makes it.

Q: In addition to your position with CBS, you have appeared on Garrison Keillhor's television show as a featured performer. How does this work into your schedule, when one job is in Nashville and the other in Minnesota?

Chet: Yes, I have worked with Garrison Keillhor on his radio show. I've only been doing that for four or five years, so it was not a problem as far as time was concerned, because all I was doing was playing my guitar, playing a few personal appearances, and some golf, and making an album now and then, so it's worked out very well. We're still good friends, and I'm sure we'll play a few more stages before the shadows get too long.

Q: In the history of your company, who do you feel is the most recorded performer(s) in any style of music? (Number of recordings--singles, albums).

Chet: Hank Snow was with RCA Victor Records for almost forty years. That's one of the longest records I know of. I'm sure Johnny Cash was with CBS for almost thirty years. He's no longer with them. I was with RCA as an artist from around 1947 'til about 1980, somewhere along there. So there have been some long careers. I've put out about sixty-five or seventy albums. I'm sure some people have done a lot more than that. I don't keep up with that.

Q: Is digital audio tape and the anticipated increase in bootleg activity a threat to the recording industry?

Chet: It just remains to be seen about DAT tape. DAT tape, of course, makes a clone. It doesn't make a copy. It makes a perfect copy, if you can say that. No one knows, I suppose, what the effect will be on the business. They are trying to keep it out of this country, out of the United States, and I don't know if that's right or wrong. I suppose people felt the same way about radios with analog tape recorders. I really don't know what the effect will be, but I don't think we can live in a world without music, so if they do hurt the business a lot, I think something would be done about it.

Q: What advice do you have for the aspiring artist who is desirous of a career in the recording industry, either as a producer or performer?

Chet: Well, it's hard to give advice to aspiring young artists. I always tell them that there are no short-cuts. You've got to learn your instrument, and study and work hard; be in the right place at the right time. And who knows what that is? You know, no one ever makes it by the same route. So, it's very hard to tell. I guess you've got to work very hard, learn the instrument, and work within your limitations, and hope for a bit of luck.

Chet Atkins Albums:

Stay Tuned: CBS—FC—39591
Sails: CBS—FC—40593
Chet Atkins Picks On The Best: RCA—LPM/LSP 3818
Lover's Guitar: RCA—LSP 4135
Greatest Hits Of The Past: RCA—AHL—1—4724
Work It Out With Chet: CBS—FC—38536

Chapter 9
Time Sharing

Time sharing is a term used in many areas of society today, in which a number of people or businesses invest in a cooperative enterprise, and while sharing the expense of purchase and maintenance, also have access to something that individually would be economically prohibitive. Recreational vehicles such as boats and airplanes, condominiums at ski resorts, mountain hideaways, and fishing cabins are all quite popular in time sharing.

In a similar fashion, jazz has developed its own time sharing process, in which top jazz performers are now dividing their time between performance with their regular groups and conducting master classes, seminars, workshops, and guest soloing with school groups. This is taking place nationwide and is proving to be one of the finest steps taken by both parties, the host school and the jazz specialist. Much of the success of this movement goes to a saxophone player and former member of the Stan Kenton band, Mr. Matt Betton, who had the foresight decades ago to see that joining the student and the professional in a learning situation could only improve the course and direction jazz should be taking. He was the founder of a group called the National Association of Jazz Educators, the membership of which today numbers thousands of teachers, students and professional musicians. At the annual convention, teachers and professionals are brought together in lecture/demonstration clinics. School and professional bands perform for the membership and serve as an inspiration to all in attendance. A kinship is formed, and philosophies are developed with the central thought of providing audiences with excellent jazz played in a professional manner.

Of course, a person must realize that if the professional musician were working on a playing schedule similar to that at the height of the big band and the bop/cool eras, this time sharing would not be possible. The young, aspiring student during those eras could only learn by listening to recordings or live performances. The professional was seldom available for counsel and guidance. The touring band could not, and probably would not, take the time to visit schools and present a coaching session or master class. The hours spent in travel and late-night gigs sapped a man of his energy and leisure time.

With the end of the eras of the big bands and be-bop, the musicians found a great deal of free time. In most cases, musicians were left without work, and since the demand for their services became almost non-existence, they had to develop secondary occupations. Fortunately for the military veterans, there was the opportunity to attend college under the veterans G. I. Bill of Rights. Musicians received education and training, and new vocations and employment. They still had the opportunity to continue their musical activity playing casual gigs.

A rather large number did, in fact, continue to pursue their profession and found work, albeit limited, in such areas as the Hollywood movie studios and subsequently in both New York and Los Angeles television studios. Still others became members of the house bands in cities such as Las Vegas and Reno, Nevada—in the resorts of Atlantic City and Miami Beach—on the cruise ships to the Caribbean and in the various countries of Europe, which rapidly became a mecca for jazz musicians. Some of the major hotels in the large metropolitan cities continued a ''live entertainment'' policy, rotating entertainment on a monthly basis. Many of the large hotel chains continue to keep a ''stable'' of entertainers under continuous contract and move them from one location to another, thereby giving performers new audiences, and audiences new entertainers.

While all of this sounds positive, it still leaves numbers of excellent musicians with little or nothing permanent in the way of work. In his interview, jazz producer Dick Gibson gives an economic comparison of earnings for jazz musicians in both Europe and Japan, and the United States. Small wonder, then, that many excellent musicians, both as individuals and in combos and bands, moved to Europe in order to continue their profession.

Through all this depression, there did arise a noteworthy development. Superstars in jazz were now available, approachable, and quite willing, for a price, to share their skills and knowledge with anyone interested, whether it was teacher or student. Bandleader Stan Kenton, along with sideman Matt Betton, formed the Stan Kenton summer workshops. A series of these were presented at various college campuses throughout the country. It was similar to the many summer music camps sponsored by colleges. In the Kenton camps, the concentration was on jazz and all it entailed, from improvisation to arranging. Many personnel from the Kenton band conducted the classes and demonstrations. For a youngster to hear the concepts of phrasing, tone production, style, blend, and range from men such as trumpeter Jimmy Maxwell, was an invaluable lesson. Being taught by someone who has "been there" inspired youngsters, who in turn took their new found skills and knowledge back to their own schools and shared the information with their peers.

Taking a lead from the symphony orchestras in the country, a number of the still-existing bands offered their services to schools on an "in residency" program. Symphony orchestras go to a college or university and spend several days in residence. Members of the orchestra conduct master classes and seminars on their particular instrument. Students are invited to "sit in" with the orchestra during rehearsals. Outstanding students are given the opportunity to conduct or solo with a major symphony. And, of course, the orchestra presents a concert or concerts for the entire school population. The bands would offer the same musical menu. Some fiscal help came from various foundations and trust funds. But here again was an opportunity for the music student to learn first hand, and often on a one-to-one basis, what the requirements of professional music really were. Some schools, realizing that the project could perhaps lose money, feel that the information given the student, which in turn will develop the program and give students a worthwhile experience, is well worth the money invested from the existing budget. It should be noted that bringing in a band for a concert or a residency, which could last from two to three days, is a costly venture. Following are the suggested prices for some of the available bands. Of course, even in this type of venture, everything is negotiable.

Count Basie Orchestra	$5,000	—	$20,000
Maynard Ferguson Band	3,000	—	12,000
Woody Herman Band	4,000	—	10,000
Lionel Hampton Band	5,000	—	15,000
Glenn Miller Orchestra	5,000	—	15,000
Les Elgart Orchestra	5,000	—	15,000
Tommy Dorsey Orchestra	3,000	—	11,500
Artie Shaw Orchestra	3,000	—	10,000

Booking agent Tom Cassidy indicates that the average ticket price for concerts by these bands is $10.00. There are many other factors to be considered. James Warrick, director of jazz studies in New Trier High School in Winnetka, Illinois, researched an article for the *Instrumentalist* magazine in which he writes: The type of event, size of auditorium, day of the week, routing, and the performers' requirements—all are contributing factors. The fee may sound high, but when divided by the number of seats in your hall, the amount seems reasonable. It is wise to always set a ticket price so that two-thirds of a full house will allow you to break even.

In addition to the availability of the bands, individual artists, many of whom are members of these same bands, are readily available to conduct seminars, workshops, clinics, and master classes. In addition, they will also perform solos with the host band, whether it be a high school band, a college band, or an all-star band. These artists have all developed a personality for this type of work. They are superb communicators. All are eager to assist and help individuals and groups. Their travel schedule is a travel agent's nightmare, having them in two locations just a day apart, or on successive days, and home again for a recording date or performance gig by the weekend. Ed Shaughnessy, "The Tonight Show" drummer, is probably the most active artist/clinician. He has six identical drum sets, available through Ludwig Industries, who ship the instruments to the various clinic locations well in advance to reduce the possibility of loss or misplacement by airlines when he travels.

These artists perform an invaluable service to jazz. Educators feel their influence on young musicians has helped to stave off the adverse forms of a pseudo jazz being performed nationwide. It is regrettable that today's rock stars cannot make themselves available. Their schedules today are what musicians schedules were like during the big band and be-bop eras. Many of today's rock stars have much to offer young musicians, in everything from recording techniques, to songwriting, to rehearsal methods and performance practices.

The critics of this practice of artists and bands working with school musicians feel that many have passed their prime. Their methods and devices are not current with the general style and theme of jazz today. Today's jazz is based upon high tech electronics. Yesterday's artists are not tuned to today's standards and methods of performance. Their prices for individual and group performances are exorbitant. How much information can one person disseminate to a group of youngsters in one day for a fee of five to ten thousand dollars? Is it merely status-seeking on the part of the host school, that artist X has lectured, demonstrated and performed with the school band? Perhaps, but even though some of the artists are moving along in years, they still have much information and inspiration to dispense to the young and interested.

Saxophonist Stan Getz (Courtesy: Thomas Cassidy, Artist Management).

The majority of the artists work through a booking agent, who negotiates fees and handles the travel arrangements. For this, the artist pays a fee to the agent. Agent's fees begin at ten percent of the lecture/performance fee. The Tom Cassidy agency lists the following fees for artists.

Stan Getz	Saxophone	$6,000	—	$12,000
Marian McPartland	Piano	5,000	—	10,000
Dizzy Gillespie	Trumpet	5,000	—	10,000
Anita O'Day	Singer	3,000	—	10,000
Ed Shaughnessy	Drums	1,500	—	3,500
Buddy DeFranco	Clarinet	1,500	—	3,500
Bill Watrous	Trombone	1,500	—	3,500

The prices vary somewhat from artist to artist, regarding travel and local expenses such as food and lodging. Some include these in their fees, while others charge these fees in addition to the seminar. A performance with the host band in addition to the seminar may also present an added fee. But all these prices are negotiable, depending on all factors, beginning with the agent and his approach. It must be remembered that agents are working primarily with and for the artist.

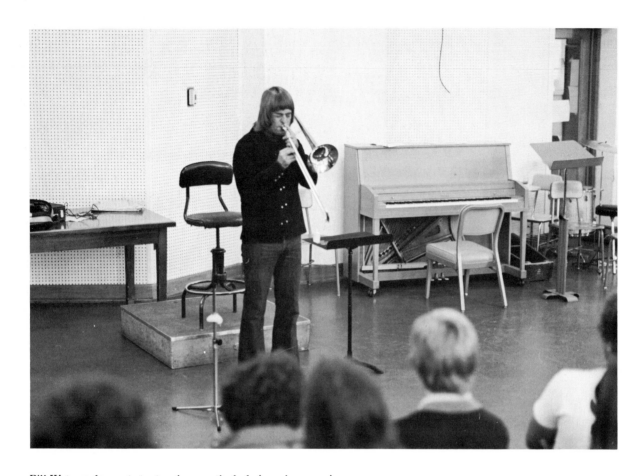

Bill Watrous demonstrates trombone methods during a brass seminar.

Additional artists who are available for clinics and concerts but for whom there are no fees available at this writing are:

Louis Bellson	Drums
Clark Terry	Trumpet
Freddie Hubbard	Trumpet
Terry Gibbs	Vibraphone
Joe Williams	Singer
Rich Matteson	Euphonium/tuba
Dianne Reeves	Singer
Tito Puente	Drums
Lionel Hampton	Band/vibraphone
Richie Cole	Saxophone
Phil Wilson	Trombone
Bobby Shew	Trumpet
Mike Vax	Trumpet
Toshiko Akiyoshi	Piano
Lew Tabakin	Saxophone
Hugh Ragin	Trumpet
Max Roach	Drums
Ed Thigpen	Drums
Sam Nestico	Arranger

The music industry, realizing the benefits to itself, has been a tremendous help in subsidizing the artist availability program. In addition to assisting with payments for travel, local expenses, and in some cases a portion of the artists personal fee, they send out artists to conventions on a simple public relations basis with no seminar, clinic or concert involved, but merely to be seen and show an interest in the school music programs. At some of the larger state and national conventions, it has been common to see artists such as Louis Bellson, drummer; the late Gene Krupa, drummer; Phil Wilson, trombonist; Ed Shaughnessy, drummer; Clark Terry, trumpeter;

Ed Thigpen makes a point during a drum master class.

Louis Bellson soloing with the Author's band during a jazz workshop.

Bill Watrous, trombonist; Red Norvo, vibraphonist; the late Woody Herman, bandleader; to name a few. The music industry, including music publishers and instrument manufacturers, realize the benefits in having artists such as these present in and around their merchandise displays. The artists, in turn, advocate the use of the manufacturer's products in both instruments, music, and various accessories. By appearing at these meetings, many contract negotiations are begun between artist and consumer. Some instrument manufacturers keep a "stable" of artists available for just such events. Artists are put on a financial retainer by the manufacturer, insuring his/her availability for conventions, seminars, guest appearances and master classes.

While some of these artists are no longer active performers in nightclubs and studios, their availability to school music programs has been an asset to the future of jazz. Young musicians who have learned from them and practiced what they have learned will be guiding the direction of jazz in the future.

Ed Shaughnessy is one of the finest drummers in professional music. In addition to his membership in Doc Severinson's "The Tonight Show" band, he is active with his own group named Energy Force. He has a full schedule of recording dates with top performers and still finds ample time to travel throughout the country conducting master classes, seminars and performing solos with college bands and the top miliary jazz bands. He has performed with the author's jazz band on four occasions including a halftime show of a football game in which he received a standing ovation with his solo on Gershwin's, "I Got Rhythm" and "Strike Up The Band".

In 1988, he won the Modern Drummer's '88 Readers' Poll. His discography includes recordings with Severinson, Basie, Clark Terry, Wes Montgomery, Charlie Parker, Charlie Ventura and Tommy Newsom. A native of Jersey City, NJ, his first notable job was as a drummer with George Shearing in a 52nd Street club in New York City in 1947. This was followed by jobs with Benny Goodman, Tommy Dorsey, Count Basie and Lucky Millinder. He joined Doc's band when "The Tonight Show" was broadcasting from New York (prior to moving to the Burbank, California studios of NBC). Residing in Woodland Hills, California, he has enjoyed twenty-four years as the most viewed drummer in the country. Experience with big bands as well as bop type combos makes him one of the best all-around drummers in music. He easily converts from playing with enormous power in a big band to a light touch with a chamber style ensemble.

The following interview gives the reader an intimate perspective of the music business from the musician's viewpoint.

Ed Shaughnessy Interview

February 12, 1988, Woodland Hills, California

Ed Shaughnessy

Q: When did you discover you had the talent to be a top drummer in your field?

Ed: I really didn't think I would be successful until I was with some pretty good professional groups, especially the Charlie Ventura band in 1949. That was a very hot group. It was as popular in its own way as perhaps Sting is today, or Wynton Marsalis. It was really a big, big name group, and in a way, I felt a little secure by the time I had gotten to work with him.

Q: The semantics involving music are rather unique. A person is a violinist or a fiddler, a saxophonist or a reedman, a pianist or a keyboardist. How do you perceive yourself, as a percussionist or as a drummer? And, why do you prefer one name over the other?

Ed: I consider myself a drummer, talking about semantics. I am a pretty good percussionist. I play some mallets, and I'm a pretty good timpanist, and I play all instruments rather well. But I still think of myself as a drummer, because I really play drum set, by far, better than I do any of the other family of the percussion field.

Q: How much practice time do you put in daily/weekly to maintain the skills you have in conjunction with your performance schedule?

Ed: I try to practice two hours a day, and I would say that I achieve that at least five days a week, sometimes more. Generally, I do that by practicing an hour at home, before I go to work at "The Tonight Show," and then I practice an hour at "The Tonight Show," because we have about an hour and a half off, and I have some silent rubber pads I put on the drum set, so I'm actually able to practice right up in the studio without bothering anyone. I try very hard to stick to my five day a week practice. I find it keeps me in good shape, and there are always new things I'm trying to work on, new challenges.

Q: What do you consider the basic schools of drumming for jazz bands? How do they differ, and who stands out as the best representatives of their styles?

Ed: Well, I think that in a way, even today in the '80's, we have drummers who tend to emulate the older style, based on the Buddy Rich/Louis Bellson approach, and this is a good style. It's perhaps not quite as contemporary as a style that might incorporate more of the be-bop style. I think that's kind of what I did, for big band drumming, in a subtle way. I was the first small band be-bop drummer who really developed into a good big band drummer, and I have that looser style that you associate more with be-bop drumming. The style of Rich and Bellson, influenced very much by Krupa, is just a little bit of a tighter style, and a much more straight ahead rhythmic style with less accenting and rhythmic accenting, in a sense breaking up of the time. You can't do too much of that in big band drumming, but I still think that is what I have contributed to

77

big band drumming. I came out of the be-bop school, and brought it into big band drumming, and yet, hopefully, still play with enough taste and time that it's a good, solid basis for whatever big band I'm playing with.

Q: What influences have rock drummers had on jazz drumming?

Ed: Not too much. It's still quite a different school of playing, and the only difference is, I think that they made a lot of jazz drummers, including myself, many years ago, realize we had to stay current with what was happening in rock and roll. Particularly in the sixties, the rock and roll drumming got much more sophisticated and actually more interesting to play. I had not paid much attention to rock and roll prior to that, because it was very what I call gorilla rock, "boom, whack, boom boom, whack, boom, whack, boom boom, whack." Boring! But then some of the great drummers, like Bernard Purdy and Al Jackson on the MoTown Records, started introducing some of these more sophisticated sixteenth-note things. Bernard Purdy, with Aretha Franklin, was a big influence on me. They got this "chooka, chooka, whacka, dooka, baka, booka, da!"—that type of feeling. It was more interesting and challenging to practice.

Q: There appear to be differences in the techniques used in playing with brushes and playing with sticks. What, in general terms, are those differences?

Ed: To play well, you have to be able to pick the brushes off the drums with more wrist motion, which is why there are not many good brush players. You don't get any bounce from the brushes. Therefore, you have to have better technique overall to play well with brushes. Not many drummers can play well with brushes. I've found that out through the years. Also, getting a good sound in rhythm with the brushes is kind of unique. It's sort of like getting a good sound on cymbals when you play rhythm. You can't play too "correct" with brushes on a snare drum. Many drummers do, and they sound too tight and too staccato. You have to sort of play the rhythm with a little more of a sideways hit or a thicker sound, more like "che, che, che, che," instead of "tick, tick, a tick," which is the biggest criticism I have of people playing brushes when I do clinics and seminars—too staccato.

Q: How have you dealt with the conception that drummers have the easiest part, in relation to the rest of the group, whether it be a big band of a combo?

Ed: Oh, I don't think that's true at all. I think that a drummer has tremendous responsibility in the way he has to play, in a big band, particularly. He has to kind of tie all the ends together, and when you say "easiest part," perhaps you're talking about strictly, literally, written part. That's not too easy, either. I get some parts at "The Tonight Show" that are just as challenging for me to play as the first trumpet player, or anybody else. I don't think it's that easy in a combo, either. If you're in a highly-charged combo, with really highly—charged jazz players, you have to contribute something that is on a level with all the horns and everybody else. So, I don't agree that drummers with either big bands or small bands have the easiest part, either in playing or in reading.

Q: How has drumming with a band changed since you got your start?

Ed: Mainly, we have to play more styles better now. The difference between now and, let's say, twenty years ago, or thirty years ago, or further back, is that you could play one way and get away with it. You can't do that anymore. Now you have to be quite good in jazz drumming, rock drumming, and Latin drumming, which are the three basic styles. We have a lot of young drummers today who play good rock and very bad jazz. They even come up on "The Tonight Show" and play with acts. This is what I keep working on at all my clinics and seminars, that we have an over-abundance of drummers who play rock well and jazz very poorly, and they do a lot of things in jazz playing that is sort of like rock and roll drumming. They play two-beats to the bar on the bass drum instead of four, and a whole bunch of other stuff that we don't have time for here. I spend a lot of my time trying to work this out at high schools and colleges throughout the country.

Q: Describe your style of playing. How has it changed over your career?

Ed: My style of playing, I think, is kind of a summation of many influences; my small band be-bop influences, and even before that, perhaps, the style of Sidney Catlet and Joe Jones, who in a way played a lighter style, not a real heavy style of playing. And then the influence of Buddy Rich, who to my mind, even though he passed on almost a year ago, was the greatest master of the drum set, as far as overall playing is concerned. This really doesn't have to do with rhythmic styles or anything else. What I'm talking about is mastery of the drum set. I used to watch him constantly as a young player, and as an older player, and I learned a lot from him. I used to talk to him about things, and although I didn't get a lot from talking to him as much as watching him, he certainly set the standard that has affected a great many of us. He showed what you could do on the drum set, and that's how I have been trying to do it, not in his way, but in my own way. He showed you there was no limit to what you could do on the drum set. I brought a lot of rock and roll into my drumming, more out of a need, because I had to, in the kind of work that I do. I find that some of it is interesting and fun to play. I like funk music more than I like what you'd call hard rock, because the rhythm is more interesting. So in my small group and my big band, we have a couple of good funk charts and funk arrangements that I enjoy playing. I'll always be a jazz player at heart. That's what I came up with, and that's what I really like the best. But I appreciate all kinds of drummers.

Q: What have been the greatest influences on your musical style?

Ed: I think not only drummers, but all musicians that I like a great deal, even sometimes symphonic things in percussion. I'm a great Stravinsky fan, and I've been influenced a great deal by his use of rhythm and percussion in his writings.

Q: How much of a drummer's (or your) success and/or satisfaction comes from being a performer (artist) rather than solely producing rhythm/music?

Ed: I would say a great deal, especially for a guy like myself. I go around and do a lot of drum solos, and I enjoy that. I wouldn't enjoy just doing drum solos and not being part of the band, but I enjoy that because it's a chance for me to do my thing, my way. On "The Tonight Show," we're very much there to perform and play for the artists that come up to the show, as well as doing our own thing from time to time, so this is a good chance for me to kind of bust loose and play whatever music I want in whatever way I want. I enjoy that. I enjoy playing solos and I enjoy interacting with bands. A lot of the college and high school bands that play well are a great deal of fun to play with, and I really enjoy that.

Q: Since you have lived and played professionally on both the East and West Coast, with both big bands and small groups in studios and clubs, describe the difference from the standpoint of musical styles, types of performances, audience expectations and the musicians' approach to jazz.

Ed: There's not a big difference. I think everything's a little more highly-charged in New York City than it is in Los Angeles. I think the approach to the music is a little more highly-charged, and I think even the audience involvement is a little more highly-charged. However, I don't think there's basically a big difference. I think perhaps it used to be more so back in the 1950 "Cool School" days; "Cool School" in California and "Hot Style" in New York, let's say typified by people like Art Blakey and Horace Silver. But even then, I mean, there were always wonderful players on both coasts, so I would say there's not a tremendously big difference in the coasts.

Q: In your opinion, having experience in both areas, how does drumming differ between combo and big band?

Ed: There's an enormous difference in the two. You have to get a much bigger sound in big band, and this does not have to do with playing louder. It has to do with getting a bigger sound. I could compare it to the good lead trumpet in a big band having to have a full sound to be successful, whereas in a small group, both the drummer and the horn player could have a smaller or thinner sound and still play very well. I find this is what a lot of drummers cannot do. They don't know how to play with a bigger sound. It definitely has to do with having a little bigger equipment, fuller tuned drums, and cymbals that are right for big band, and perhaps different than you'd use in small band, and very, very much the matching up of the drum set to the rhythmic pulsation. In a big band you need a little more bass drum, rhythmic bass drum, like in 4/4, you have to play some rhythmic bass drum. It should be felt, not heard, but at the same time, that's the big difference. There are many more good combo drummers than there are big band drummers. I travel the country a lot, and I can say that quite accurately. I hear a lot of good combo drummers and very few good big band drummers. I think it takes quite awhile to develop into one. It certainly took me quite awhile.

Q: How much importance do you place upon the rapport between the drummer and the bandleader?

Ed: I think it's very important. I have a good rapport with Doc Severinsen and he with me. I think, between us, that helps get tempos right and everything else. Neither one of us feels we're perfect. I think that's the key to the success of it. Doc doesn't think he always hits the exact right tempo, and I'm not going to say I hit the exact right tempo all the time either. Although he depends a lot on me to suggest the right tempo, neither one of us is afraid to make a slight change during the first eight bars or so of a tune that we feel either one of us has not beat off properly. I think this is important. There's nothing that says it's carved in stone, that you have to stay at exactly the same tempo for the first eight or sixteen bars. It's better to get it into the right groove for the rest of the tune, if you need to adjust slightly up or slight down in tempo.

Q: What is the role of the rhythm section (piano, bass, drums, guitar) as an entity in itself and as a unit for a band?

Ed: To provide a good foundation, whether that's big band or small band. I really look upon my job, except for when I play solos, as trying to make the soloists in front be comfortable, and in a big band, to make the group ensemble sound comfortable, and soloists comfortable also. This has to do with keeping your ego in the right place, so that you play for other people when that's your job, and not for yourself alone.

Q: Discuss the value and method of reading music today, compared to the early days of jazz.

Ed: It's much more difficult today, and much more needed. Particularly in the rock and funk area, some of the stuff that you get is very complex, a lot of mixed-up sixteenth-note patterns. Even some of the rhythmic patterns they want you to play between snare drum and bass drum and rhythm cymbals are very difficult. I get a lot of these parts on "The Tonight Show," and they're very, very difficult, compared to earlier years of jazz arrangements only. So reading is more important than ever.

Q: What equipment changes have there been in terms of kinds of percussion instruments which seem standard in today's performance requirements?

Ed: I guess the difference would be that you might have to have a few extra tom-toms in drum sets so that you run the gamut for rock and roll breaks and things from high-pitch to low-pitch toms. You don't get away with it as well on a four or five-piece drum set. You can play on those, but I would say it would be good to have a few extra toms so that you have the overall tonal range and everything, and I wouldn't say that there's a heck of a lot of difference, except everything's much heavier, in terms of weight of the stand, because rock-and-rollers demanded that. They play so very hard.

Q: What kind, if any, mallet work is expected of you?

Ed: I don't have much mallet work. Occasionally I play a note or two on a tympani or something like that, but basically, I don't take calls on percussion anymore, since I don't want to spend the time trying to keep my mallet work up. I'm too interested in trying to keep on developing my drum set. This is my strength, the thing I do best. Therefore, although I used to work as a percussionist in New York years ago, I have not accepted work as a percussionist for a long time. I feel if I do, I want to do it at my best, and I don't want to spend the hours a day needed for mallets.

Ed Shaughnessy playing a solo with The Tonight Show Orchestra (Courtesy: Thomas Cassidy, Artist Management).

Q: When guests come on ''The Tonight Show'' and bring their own arrangements, which ones have the best charts and what makes the arrangement effective?

Ed: People who bring charts up that are well-written and clear, like Tony Bennett and B.B. King and people like that, are some of our best performers. And particularly, what makes the arrangement effective is that it has been played before, so we don't have to correct all the wrong notes made on an arrangement freshly copied the night before. This takes an enormous amount of our time at rehearsal, when people have brand new charts that have never been played before. It isn't that they're so hard to play. It's that there are a lot of wrong copy notes because the poor copyist probably got it at three a.m., and had to have it done by nine, or something. So a good, clear, definitive copy of an arrangement, with the artist knowing exactly what he wants—that's what makes everything good.

Q: In recent years, you have been doing a number of clinics and seminars on campuses throughout the country. In your teaching, what do you emphasize, and how would you describe your teaching style/procedure?

Ed: I emphasize rhythm a great deal. The last few years, I've spent much more time on how to play good rhythm than on how to hold the sticks and achieve a great deal of technique, because I find the weakest area in rhythm, and if I don't do that job when I get to a college or high school, I don't feel like I'm doing my job right. In my teaching style and procedure, I incorporate a lot of contemporary music. I carry tapes with me, with my own tape player. I put this through a sound system and develop living examples of how you play jazz, rock, and Latin, with most emphasis being on jazz, because this is what people do not have today. They don't have many examples to listen to or observe. It's not their fault. It's just that MTV doesn't teach you how to play with Count Basie.

Q: Besides music, what other personal achievements have given you pride?

Ed: Without a doubt, my family. I think that the raising of our two boys and doing family activities have been the things that have given me the most pride, and also the success of many of my students, that used to study with me back in New York. I have many people, like John Dietrich playing with the great country rock group, Restless Heart, and Steve Schaefer out here, who studied with me awhile in New York, who's probably our busiest Hollywood drummer—different people like that, who have gone on to do well. And many of my other guys, who maybe haven't become famous but are making a good living. That makes me feel really good. But, without a doubt, my family, first of all, has been the most important thing. We lost our oldest son in 1984 to a reckless driver. However, I like to refer to the years we raised both our boys as very happy years, because luckily we raised them over a period of eighteen years. My younger son, Dan, who is now nineteen, is a business major and sophomore at Cal State Northridge. He's a really fine fellow. My family times are still important. Luckily, Dan has chosen to live at home, and I enjoy still having him in the house. He and I are both avid tennis players, and share a lot of other interests together.

Q: What do you want to accomplish professionally in the years to come?

Ed: I just want to keep trying to play better. I feel like I can always play better, and I think bit by bit it's been coming, especially over the last couple of years. I seem to get more focused on things I want to do, and I hope I'll do maybe another video or two that will be helpful to people. I do have a video now that people like a lot, and it has sold quite well. I'm looking forward to teaching much more in the years to come, particularly when "The Tonight Show" stops. I'm a lucky guy, in that I look forward to that period of my life when I can teach more, because I'll have more time for it.

Q: What advice can you offer to the aspiring young musician who wants to make music performance a life's vocation?

Ed: Hard work and dedication are still the answer, just like when I started. I'm not exaggerating when I say that many days I practiced six hours a day for a very long time when I was young. I've always continued to practice, and I really believe that the dedication and hard work is what really pays off in the long run. I even had some students that I wanted to tell, "I think you ought to go into some other business," and because they were dedicated and hard-working, they showed me that even people that don't have a heck of a lot of basic talent can achieve quite a bit in the business. That was a good lesson to me as a teacher. I'm always glad that I stayed with them and didn't discourage them, because they showed me that dedication and hard work, even without a lot of God-given talent, can at least make them a working musician who can earn a decent living, and I think that's terrific. The main thing next to that is, "Keep your nose clean." I particularly want to say, "Avoid drugs," because we have seen so many wonderful young musicians either die or ruin their health, their lives, their families, and everything else. Drugs are very insidious, and I've seen a lot of drug use in my time. I think because I lost two good friends to drug use, to overdoses, when I was young, it always frightened me a great deal, and I was able to stay away from it. I want to offer that advice to young musicians. Many people make young people feel that this is the "hip" way to go. It is definitely not the

Ed Shaughnessy with complete drum set (Courtesy: Thomas Cassidy, Artist Management).

"hip" way to go, and is one of the most dangerous things for a young person to get involved in. I like to leave young people with the advice that getting high on life and getting high on music are the two greatest highs you can get. And getting high on your family and all the good values of home and family, without a doubt, beats the heck out of all that other stuff.

Ed Shaughnessy Recording List:

Doc Severinsen	Brass Roots	RCA 4522
Count Basie	Broadway-Basie's Way	Command 905
George Benson	The Other Side of Abbey Road	A&M 3028
Wes Montgomery	Road Song	A&M 3012
Quincy Jones	Golden Boy	Mercury 20938
Charlie Ventura	In Concert	Gene Norman 102
Charlie Parker	Parker w/Friends	Blue Parrot-AR704

Chapter 10
Concerts and Festivals

The concept of putting jazz on a concert stage originated with one of the pioneers of the big band movement, Paul Whiteman. In 1924, in Aeolian Hall in New York City, he presented what historians consider the first bona fide jazz concert. It included compositions such as "The Livery Stable Blues," a popular Dixieland number. The program culminated with George Gershwin playing the piano solo to his historic orchestral jazz composition, "Rhapsody in Blue."

James Warrick (left) and Dizzy Gillespie at the New Trier High School Jazz Festival (Courtesy: James Warrick Collection).

The time immediately following this historic event became known as the era of the big bands, also known as dance bands. Dancing became the popular pastime of Americans. They flocked to the dance halls and ballrooms across the country with the same fervor that today's health enthusiasts take to the streets jogging and biking.

Jazz concerts were not in vogue at the time, and went into a hiatus. Not until 1944 was the idea of a jazz concert proposed. Then it was under the guidance of jazz promoter Norman Granz, who brought it into the musical spotlight. Labeled "Jazz at the Philharmonic" and later listed simply as JATP, Granz toured the concert halls throughout the country, presenting the finest jazz musicians together in ensembles that made jazz history and helped to herald and popularize the be-bop and cool periods. (Some critics, however, complained that these JATP concerts were merely high-powered jam sessions.) In addition to his concert enterprise, Granz also owned Verve Records. He recorded the concerts live, and from these recordings produced long-playing records of the choice selections from a concert. In 1960, he sold Verve Records to MGM for $2,750,000 and moved to Switzerland. Possibly because he became irritated by competition, he left this country and began similar activities in Europe.

In 1954, an energetic young jazz promoter named George Wein formulated what was to become one of the world's best-known and most well-attended jazz festivals, in Newport, Rhode Island. The Newport festivals were an annual bash for both musicians and audiences. Attendance numbered in the thousands. Unfortunately, these large numbers caused its eventual demise, by turning a successful musical presentation into a riot. Wein then moved his festival to New York City, where it met with tremendous success. In the 1980's, his festivals were called the Kool Jazz Festivals and were in part sponsored by a tobacco company. Kool festivals were also presented in Cleveland, Cincinnati, Baltimore, Chicago, St. Louis, Detroit and Houston. The structure was always the same; hire jazz stars, put them on a stage, let them demonstrate their individual skills and present continuous music for the duration of the festival. At some of the festivals, complete bands were hired to perform.

Festivals as a financial enterprise, when properly administered, can be an economic boon to the organizer/producer. In one particular year, (exact year unavailable), JATP grossed about five million dollars.

Today, festivals occur year round, with the major thrust during the spring, summer and early fall months, depending on geographic locations. Jazz buffs can plan their spring, summer, or fall vacations to coincide with festivals from coast to coast, including Canada and Europe. Many of these festivals have adopted the description ''traditional jazz festivals'' or Dixieland festivals. Besides the Kool festivals which primarily encompass the Eastern states, numerous Midwest and West coast festivals have become quite popular with vacationers. The festival at Sacramento is a typical example of how these are organized. It is possibly one of the largest of the traditional jazz festivals. Total attendance numbers in the thousands, but each site is in a small club or auditorium. The performances are spread throughout the city, so transportation from site to site is necessary. A large number of bands are contracted and appear as complete units. Festival-goers can pay a daily fee or a festival fee which entitles them to admittance to all performance sites. The music at each location is continuous from about 10:00 A.M. 'til about 1:00 A.M. Following are some additional festivals.

Sparks, Nevada: Johnny Ascauga's Nugget Casino
Telluride, Colorado: Telluride Jazz Festival
San Francisco Peninsula: Rotary Jazz Festival
Rock Island, Illinois: Bix Beiderbecke Jazz Fest
Stockton, California: Jazz Festival
Los Angeles, California: L.A. Classic Labor Day Jazz Festival
Helena, Montana: Montana Traditional Jazz Festival
New Orleans, Louisiana: Traditional Jazz Festival

The Music Staff at the Arizona Jazz Festival. Left to right: Glenn Shull, trombone; Larry Lashley, bass; Gil Garcia, trumpet; Bob Nisbett, piano; Mic Hardin, reeds; Otto Werner, drums.

Bands come from all over the country to participate in these festivals. Their names reflect their style, their geographic location or sometimes their leader's nickname. Typical examples include the Side Street Strutters from Phoenix, Arizona and the Southern Comfort Band from Washington D.C. Following is a list of bands and solo artists appearing at the annual Montana Jazz Festival:

Uptown-Lowtown	Seattle, Washington
Hot Frogs Jumpin' Jazz Band	Hollywood, California
Last Chance Dixieland Band	Helena, Montana
Good Time Jazz Band	Kalispell, Montana
Golden Gate Jazz Band	San Francisco, California
Wild Rose Dixieland Band	Calgary, Alberta, Canada
Hume Street Preservation Band	Aberdeen, Washington
Big Bear Jazz Band	State Center, Iowa
The Tarnished Six	Bellefonte, Pennsylvania
Tri-City Jazz Band	Richland, Washington
Flathead Ragtimers	Whitefish, Montana
Arizona Classic Jazz Band	Phoenix, Arizona
Dixieland North	Bismarck, North Dakota
Arthur Duncan	Van Nuys, California
Pauline Filby	London, England
Ernie Carson	Atlanta, Georgia

Unlike rock concerts which are staged in stadiums, field houses or arenas capable of holding audiences numbering in the tens of thousands, present day jazz festivals are held in intimate nightclub settings. If more room is needed, theaters or auditoriums are utilized. The format is to have continuous music in several locations throughout the day and evening, ending around midnight. The festivals generally are scheduled for three days. Those attending purchase a festival pass which allows them into any session in any location at any time. Festival producers supplement revenues by selling programs, T-shirts, and various memorabilia. Food and beverage sales are handled by the club owners at the various locations. The latter procedure aids both the festival producer and the club owner.

Gibson Jazz Poster

Europe became very interested in jazz following World War II. Since that time, many jazz artists have migrated there to make their homes. The rationale for this move was that Europe was much more receptive to jazz than the United States, which was undergoing a change to rock and roll. Norman Granz began producing festivals all over Europe. England and France were the most receptive, but countries such as the Netherlands, Germany, and Spain were also quite hospitable. However, in recent years, Europeans have not been overly enthusiastic about concerts and festivals. Granz states that Scandinavia is all but finished with jazz concerts, favoring rock instead. In Germany, only four or five cities show any interest. France and England are only receptive in Paris and London. The top English festival was held on the grounds of Beaulieu Abbey, in front of Lord Montaguis' estate. Unfortunately, the fans, in all their enthusiasm, were like fans of winners at championship baseball and football games in this country. Instead of tearing up the turf and goal posts, they proceeded to take apart the bandstand in quest of souvenirs, thereby causing a riot.

The newest innovation in these festivals is an occasion called a jazz party. There are several of these in existence throughout the country. Their origin can be traced to jazz producer Dick Gibson (see following interview). In this jazz party, which is held annually during the Labor Day weekend, he presents seventy to seventy-five of the nation's leading jazz artists. Gibson arranges them in groups to play continuous sets of an hour each. Located in Denver at one of the city's hotels, his jazz party attracts listeners from Europe, South America, and the Orient, as well as Canada and the fifty states. A large majority of his clientele are repeat customers.

Dick Gibson is one of the few premier jazz producers in this country. He has taken up where Norman Granz left off. He developed the jazz party concert, which today is being emulated in various parts of the nation. The first jazz party was held in Aspen, Colorado. The audience was very small, but he went through with the party, nevertheless. A short time later he moved the party to the prestigious Broadmoor Hotel in Colorado Springs. He has since moved it to Denver, where he will continue until such time as he feels a new location is needed. His staff consists of himself and his wife, Maddie. They call their organization Gibson Jazz. He dislikes having it referred to as Dick Gibson's jazz party or concert. In observing their operation, it becomes immediately apparent that it is a joint effort. Prior to the party or a concert, additional help is used in marketing and production. In recent years, they bought and sold a jazz radio station. Producing jazz parties and concerts and managing a radio station were too much for just two people.

A native of Mobile, Alabama, Gibson has had a varied and exciting number of careers, from football coach, to college professor, to being a jazz producer. An invitation to perform at a Gibson jazz party or jazz concert is a mark of success in the jazz profession. Following is an interview with a person to whom the music world has given the name, "Jazz Man."

Dick Gibson Interview

April 6, 1988, Denver, Colorado

Dick and Maddie Gibson

Dick and Maddie Gibson

Q: Dick, in the music world you are listed as a jazz producer. First of all, tell us what, in your estimation, is a jazz producer?

Dick: Well, I'd never really thought of it, but I guess he's a fellow that can produce live jazz and recorded jazz. And I only talk to people who make records, and I'm somewhat responsible for some jazz albums that are made, because I give recommendations and ideas to people who make records. But fundamentally, I produce live jazz shows, jazz parties, and concerts.

Q: How did you initially get into this area of music?

Dick: When I was at the University of Alabama, for a year I had access to the student activity fund to hire big bands. So, in 1946, I'd hire Stan Kenton, Tommy Dorsey, and whoever, and they'd come to the University of Alabama. Every college does that. And I got a taste for that. I'd done a few little things in Mobile earlier, but they were very amateurish. That's forty-two years ago, and then I did some things when I lived in New York. And the jazz parties, which I seem to be pretty much known for now all over the world, there are now fifty-four jazz parties that are, in effect, spinoffs of ours, in one way or another, directly or indirectly, and that started twenty-five years ago here in Denver. Maddie and I were talking one night, and Denver wasn't too heavy in jazz. It's not a jazz town. And we were thinking about what we missed about New York. We missed the ocean and the jazz, and I said to Maddie, " I can't do anything about the ocean, but I've got an idea," and we decided to give a private jazz party, and we'd assemble musicians and we'd try to cover the cost of it. It was conceived as non-profit and has remained non-profit.

Q: In your student days, you hired bands, full bands like Kenton and Dorsey, but today, you're going with individuals and comprising what we call the Dick Gibson bands. When did you decide to make that change, as literally a booking agent, from a university with big bands, to small groups with individual stars?

Dick: About thirty years ago in New York, when I did it a few times—small little things. In what I really wanted to hear, it's always been personal, and I just hoped that enough people would go along with my ideas to make them worthwhile. I never could hear groups, as groups, that I wanted to hear. The most common thing in the world is, "so and so and his all stars," and his all stars are very often the first five guys he could pick up at the union hall that would work the cheapest. There are some good groups, but there are always clunkers in these all-star bands. I wanted to hear certain people together, and I started doing that, and it worked, and now an awful lot of people are doing that.

Q: In going back to the days of Norman Granz and his Jazz at the Philharmonic, would you say he was the forerunner of this type of activity with jazz concerts by small ensembles of select musicians?

Dick: Certainly. I don't even know who did it before Norman, but he certainly did it best. He started in the mid-40's with his Jazz at the Philharmonic. And he would hire all stars. He'd hire individuals and put them together in a group. I never was aware of that in those terms, but looking at it truthfully and objectively, he did pre-date me with that. Oddly enough, I wasn't influenced by that at the time. I wasn't aware of it that much.

Q: On Norman Granz's concerts, he did LP records, recorded the whole thing, and then sold them as Jazz at the Philharmonic recordings. You have never delved into that. Why not?

Dick: Well, I just like to hear them play. It's always been a lot of trouble when you get into recording. You have to deal with contracts and agents, and one year, I let MPS-BASF, the German record company, record our 1971 jazz party. It's a German company, Bayer. They hired RCA technicians, and they came out to the Broadmoor in 1971 and recorded the Jazz Party, and then they had a boxed set of three LP's for Europe. I never did like it very much. I didn't like what they picked—but that was their choice. I don't know how they sold. We got fraudulent reports from them. It no longer exists, but they cheated us, and I don't mind that being in print.

Q: You have a fine track record of selecting the right combinations of people to perform on your various concerts and jazz parties. How do you go about it? Is there any formula that you use in selecting this musician to play with that musician?

Dick: No, you can't have a formula really. The first thing I think about is a jazz band. I put together ten-piece jazz bands. That's a predilection of mine, and the reason is because it's got enough variety to satisfy me, it doesn't have too many people to where in a performance you can't give them all a solo, and it's enough to generate some power, some long lines, when you want a full band number. So you've got the ability to feature variety. If you have a seventeen-piece band, that's a big band. That's not what I do, and you couldn't give them all solos, and a really great ten-piece band can generate almost the same power.

Q: You're not considering so many reed players versus so many brass players are you?

Dick: No, it'll vary. Sometimes I'll have two trumpets, two trombones, and three reeds, and sometimes it'll be one trumpet, one trombone and five reeds, with a rhythm section. Then if you've got a guitar in there with the piano, bass, and drums, you might have eleven.

Q: Your jazz party originated or started at the Broadmoor Hotel in Colorado Springs?

Dick: No, it began in the Jerome Hotel in Aspen, in 1963. We had ten musicians. I forget now what it cost us, but maybe it was going to cost around $8,000, so we were going to look for the number of people it would take at $25 or $50 a piece, to pay for it. Maddie and I went up and down the street, getting people by the throat, "Will you please come to our jazz party?" And, of course, no one had ever heard of a jazz party, and so it was a hard thing to convey. And, I think our first party in the Jerome had sixty-five or seventy guests. We didn't lose much. We've never broken even on a jazz party in twenty-five years. We budget to break even, and then there's always something we don't anticipate.

Q: Is Gibson Jazz primarily Maddie and yourself?

Dick: Totally.

Q: Do you have a staff of people to assist?

Dick: No.

Q: How can you do this?

Dick: Well, we've been asked that a thousand times. It's just that we know how. I can't give you any other reason than that. We pioneered it, and evolved it, and Maddie is an extremely disciplined worker at this. She does a tremendous amount of work. I always get peeved when people call it the Dick Gibson Jazz Party, because it's the Dick and Maddie Gibson Jazz Party. She does as much work as I. We talk together about who we're going to hire this year. Last year, 1987, was our twenty-fifth anniversary. We had seventy-one musicians, all hired individually, and let me tell you, that is a hell of a lot of individual musicians.

Q: Let's say you're going to plan your next jazz party. First of all, what would be the format? Selecting the musicians, selecting the site?

Dick: The site comes first. You stick with the site 'til you decide you're going to move. We were in Aspen five years and in Vail three years, at the Broadmoor eleven years. We're now in the Fairmont hotel here in Denver. We just move it around when it seems to have run its course somewhere. And as for who you hire, if you're going to put together a jazz band, you want to think—there is one curious thing most people don't know, but you want to give an extra amount of thought believe it or not, to your trumpet and bass. That wouldn't occur to a lot of people. Of course you have to have the piano. But for the thing to swing, you have to have a lead trumpet, 'cause a ten-piece jazz band is a huge jazz band. It doesn't even exist in nature, you might say. You can't go anywhere and hear a ten-piece jazz band. And therefore, you put a tremendous premium on your lead trumpet, because jazz, as you know, is a tapestry in music, and in a really great jazz band, everybody else but the trumpet is playing the harmony parts. So the stronger the lead is, the easier it is to play a harmony part. You've got to have a center pole for your tent. So the first person you really think about is your lead trumpet, and then you've got to have a great drummer, because a jazz band cannot be better than its drummer. It can be better than its clarinet player, or better than its tenor, if it's really fine in all of its other parts. It can actually supersede, in excellence, a given player. It cannot be better than its drummer. He determines the upper limits of how good the band can be. So, you pay a lot of attention to your lead trumpet, your drummer, and your piano. Then though, you spend a lot of time wondering what bass to put with that, because they're the bottom of the sound, and the bass enriches the sound of every other thing in that band. And somehow, I just learned, if you've got a trumpeter and a bass that are not quite in some form of sync, your band tends to fall apart.

Q: What was your role in the organization, development, and activities of a group called "The World's Greatest Jazz Band"?

Dick: I owned it. I put it together, and gave it that unearthly name that they all hated. It was the greatest band of its kind in the world. The original band that we launched in '68 at the Riverboat in New York included Hank Lawson and Billy Butterfield on trumpets, Lou McGarrity and Carl Fontana on trombones, Bud Freeman on tenor, and Bob Wilbur on soprano. The rhythm section had Clancy Hayes on banjo. The banjo really didn't work. It's a half a tone off, even when it's in tune. The rhythm was Ralph Sutton, piano, Bob Haggert, bass, and Morey Feld on drums. The band evolved a little bit over the relatively few years of its existence. We traveled over the world, and really did fairly well. Jazz was deader than hell in 1968, 1969, 1970. That was the great Woodstock rock years in New York, which was our home base. I commuted from Denver. I lived back there in a little suite in the Roosevelt Hotel, but I'd come home once a month, and then once a month I'd take Maddie and the children back there for a week-end. It was quite a project. It was meant to try and turn jazz around, but the times were just difficult. You could have had Jesus and the disciples in the band in 1969, and you wouldn't have gotten any attention.

Q: Your background has music in it. You were a singer, and actually at one time had recording contracts. How did that help you, do you feel, in your activities today?

Dick: Oh, I don't know. I've just always been music-oriented. I was born and reared in Mobile, and around the corner from my home, on Carolina Avenue, on this little street in Mobile, was a black settlement of homes. Mobile's a very old city, and a lot of people in those homes were the gardeners or the cooks of maybe the surrounding sixteen to eighteen blocks. And in one of the homes was a Mr. Johnson, who was the straw boss of a band, the Excelsior Firemen's Marching Band of Mobile. It still exists. Mr. Johnson's son, Joe John, was my age. We were both five and six years old. Mobile was like all towns in America then. I'm talking like 1930. It was very safe, so a kid could wander around without anybody being worried. There might have been a murder a year in Mobile. I mean it was a safe town, and I was a prodigy. When I was four, I was on the radio with a guy named Easy Al Treadway. I always wondered why he smelled funny. When I got to be twelve, I remembered this, and I realized that he was always drunk. But I didn't know what booze smelled like at four. Nobody drank in my family. My father had gone to New York and my mother had gone to Chicago. I was living with my grandparents. And, so, I was a prodigy, and I was on the radio, and people would call and say, "Ask him to spell 'originality,' " or things like this, or "Ask him to multiply 13 by 17 by 19." That's 4,199. They'd call in with all kinds of questions. When I was five, Mr. Johnson was the head of this band. It was the only band in Mobile that swung in the Mardi Gras parades. My great-grandfather and another man started Mardi Gras in the United States in Mobile. New Orleans picked it up four years later from Mobile. And the term for that music, "swing," hadn't been invented. And I'd go around the corner and play marbles all day with Joe John, who was my best friend. Every black jazz musician that would ever come through Mobile in those days would stop off at Mr. Johnson's home. So, I'd stay around these jam sessions 'til it got dark. My grandparents weren't worried. They knew where I was. And then I'd wander home late, but by the time I'm six years old, I'm hooked on jazz. I sat on Leadbelly's knee when I was seven years old, and I learned years later he was hiding out from the cops at the time. He'd escaped from the penitentiary in Louisiana. He went to the penitentiary twice for murder. So I really had jazz roots at six years of age. I just was around it, and they all called me—it sounds like a B movie—but they called me "White Boy." I don't think most of them knew my name, but that was my world. I was hooked at six, and now I'm sixty-two, so I've been hooked on jazz for fifty-six years. I started singing in high school with Bill Legman's "Have a Tampa Cigar" Band. They paid him a hundred bucks a year to use that name. I had a deep voice and it changed down. But I sang in this band, and I knew all the tunes, had a sense of melody and a sense of swing, and sense of time. I still have it. So, I don't know how much that helped me. It's like the jazz musicians have an ear, (and I don't have to tell you that some people don't!), and that ear that you have for music is formed very early, and no one has a clue what forms it in this guy, and not in that guy.

Q: Going back to your days at the university, weren't you also a football star?

Dick: I was not a star. I played on a great team. We played in two Sugar Bowls and a Rose Bowl, but I was not a star.

Q: Weren't you also in the coaching profession?

Dick: I stayed on and coached football at Alabama for three years in the late '40's as an assistant coach, and then decided I didn't want to be a coach. That wasn't to be my life. I went to New York on New Year's Day, 1950. I just moved up there with no job prospects. I'd been an assistant professor of creative writing, and running the white rat lab in the psychology department at the University of Alabama, and coaching football. I thought, "What the hell am I doing?" and I just pulled up and left that environment.

Q: With all your background, experience, and your association with the world's greatest jazz musicians, what, in your opinion, is the future of jazz? Are we going to have nostalgia and go back to jazz, or is it going to go in a new and different direction?

Dick: Well, it's already gone in different and, to me, impossible, directions. I have very little feeling for fusion. Fusion has many more rock characteristics than jazz characteristics. It was invented by A & R men in studios. Jazz has a little snob appeal to it. You run into kids today, and they'll say "Charlie's into jazz!" They're giving him a compliment. One of them's into jazz, and he likes fusion, because it sounds like what he's used to. He's into jazz, but he's still hearing his amplifiers and his simple riffs. I think its aptly named, because I don't think anybody'll ever pay to hear it. Jazz is just lost out there with the young people. They don't know what it is or where it is. They go to these jazz things, and some of these bands are straight ahead rock, absolutely straight ahead rock, and they cheer just as much. They don't know it isn't jazz. So I don't know about nostalgia. I get called a purist, and I say, "Well, that's like calling a guy, a baseball fan, a purist because he says there ought to be three outs instead of four. You ought to catch the ball on the fly instead of on the first bounce." I mean, something is or isn't what it is, and jazz is lost out there, and the older guys, the really great players, are dying. But now there is a resurgence of young players that are really good, for the first time in a generation, so I think jazz has got a very good chance. There's a million kids taking jazz for credit in junior high school, high school, junior colleges, colleges, universities, music schools and graduate schools. And if you go back seven years, that million might have been 200,000, so jazz is moving, except it's got to find a center again.

Q: What advice do you have for somebody that wants to start out as a jazz producer?

Dick: Well, it's very hard, as you know, as a teacher. Music is a sequence of sounds, and music is its own thing, and music is real, and music is hard. If everything, every sound was music, noise would be music. Music has a structure. Jazz should be experimental, but where it lost its way is it still promulgates experiments that fail. Nothing wrong with trying something, but if it doesn't work, it isn't dropped in jazz. It gets a little splinter of adherents, who can't hear a melody, or who can't hear any kind of linear progression, or whatever. Just to follow my lead is not very lucrative. I don't know why anybody would want to. The basis is getting people who can play, and also having a sense of who can play together. I know who can play together. Also, another thing that's very important is—these fellows travel the world over, and there may be 250 to 300 true great jazz musicians in the world out of five billion people. But a lot of these guys don't like a lot of these guys. They're like scorpions in a bottle. I'm one of the tribe. It's a tribe, and you've got to really know who hates who, because it's a collaborative music, and if you've got a trumpet player in a band, and a bass player, and they hate each other (and I could give you some examples but I won't), it doesn't work quite as well. It just doesn't swing quite as well. So, you really have to know your subject down to the ground to do it right. What trumpet do you put with that trombone? Most people have never heard these people play together, and they're coming up to me every day of my life saying, "Have you ever heard so-and-so? Well, he's fantastic!" And they're talking about some mediocre player. How do I know that? Because I've heard him play. Financially, there's not much money in jazz, for record companies, or for me. I do it my own way. We've never made any money in jazz. We made money on our concerts, but that's an income. In terms of real money, I imagine my concerts are the most profitable jazz concerts in the country. I almost said in the world, but jazz is so popular in Europe and Japan, that I'm sure there are people over there that actually make a million dollars on jazz. There are no jazz producers I know of doing the same thing I'm doing. They don't know how. But they hire Benny Carter. Somebody in Japan hired Benny last year, and he rounded up seven guys, and went over there—I won't get into what they paid Benny—and he plays four concerts in one week over there. In Tokyo, there were seventy-thousand people in attendance; in Osaka, seventy-thousand people, in Yokohama, eighty-thousand people, and in another city, eighty-thousand people. Japan is the hottest jazz market in the world by far. I bring Benny Carter to the Paramount Theater here in Denver to one of my concerts, and I can't tell you how many tickets Benny expressly sells, in other words, how many fewer tickets would we sell if we had Joe Hogomoga on the alto instead of the great Benny Carter, but I'll bet you Benny doesn't sell over two or three hundred tickets. We are a junk food music country. The great jazz musicians make their living in Europe, in Japan, in Brazil, and places like that. They will work for a third of the year, and make easily three-fourths of their income for the year. And they'll work in America two-thirds of the year, and hopefully make a fourth of their income. Don't ever urge anybody to go into jazz promotion to make a lot of money. I've tried to, but I certainly haven't. Norman made a lot of money, and George Wein has made a lot of money, I think, with his Newport concerts, and maybe Carl Jefferson is doing fairly well with Concord Jazz Records. I don't know that, but I think so, but other than that, it's a graveyard for financially ambitious people.

Q: Dick, you do have a little bit of leisure time. What are your hobbies? How do you spend your leisure time? What do you enjoy doing?

Dick: Well I do a little writing, and I'm a rug collector, antique rugs, and I also collect cloisonné. I read extensively in mathematics and jazz. I enjoy reading.

Q: Do you and Maddie travel very much?

Dick: Maddie and I hardly travel at all. We're pretty much home bodies unless we're doing something. People think of us as very, very active, because when they see us or hear about us when we're doing something public. But now, we won't go anywhere. We'll sit here for three weeks without going to the store. There's quite a bit of time taken up by my antique rug collection and antique cloisonné collection. I'm always roaming through the shops. But the days fill up. We're not bored. We consider ourselves active in a personal way.

Appendix A: Study Guides

Following are two study guides for the jazz history student. They are designed to encompass the eras of jazz in two chronological phases. Included are names of people that had specific functions in the development. Also included are subjects, places and events which were important throughout history and which contributed important factors to the continual changes that took place in the short time jazz has been in existence.

Study Guide for Mid-Term Examination

In order to insure success on the mid-term examination, the student should be familiar with the following material.

The mid-term examination will include questions on the following eras of jazz. Know the approximate date for each.

> Roots of jazz from Africa to the United States
> The Work Song
> Minstrelsy
> Ragtime
> Dixieland

Know the means by which jazz was spread around the country and the world.

Know the meaning of the following terms associated with jazz:

double entendre	race recordings
blue notes	scat singing
city blues	olio
rural blues	patting juba
chord progression (blues)	spirituals
tailgate trombone	acoustical recordings
syncopation	front line
boogie woogie	back line
break	improvisation
stoptime	jam session
song form (AABA)	uptown negro
ragtime form (ABCD)	downtown negro
cutting contest	T.O.B.A.
call & response	rent party
Dixieland	house hop
a. New Orleans	stride
b. Chicago	walkaround
field holler	tag ending
head arrangements	introduction

Be able to associate each of the following dances with an era of jazz:

ring shout	Lindy hop
cakewalk	black bottom
quadrille	Charleston

Know the components of jazz, and the order of their importance in both classical music and jazz.

Be able to associate the following people with a specific style and/or era of jazz:

Master drummer	Baby Dodds	James R. Europe	Ma Rainey
W. C. Handy	Mr. Bones	King Oliver	Wingy Manone
Stephen Foster	Mr. Tambo	Papa Celestin	John Starck
Scott Joplin	Interlocutor	Kid Ory	Thomas Edison
Jelly Roll Morton	Leadbelly	Lil Hardin	Alphonse Picou
Tom Turpin	Fats Waller	Bessie Smith	Sidney Bechet
James P. Johnson	Eubie Blake	Lizzie Miles	Johnny St. Cyr

Know the members of the "Austin High Gang" and the instruments which they played.

Be familiar with the products of the following record companies:

Pace-Black Swan
Gennett
OKEH
Victor
Edison
Columbia

Know the four major cities credited with the development of jazz to this point in its history, and why they were important.

Know the following places important in jazz history:

Congo Square   Harlem
Africa's Gold Coast   Los Angeles
West Indies   Chicago
New Orleans   Kansas City
Storyville   Austin High School
Mississippi River   Canal Street

Know the names of the leading minstrel shows.

Know the instruments used in jazz up to this time.

Know the classical composers who attempted to write ragtime.

Following are a number of Dixieland bands that were important to the development of that particular era. Know the names of the leaders.

Red Hot Peppers—Jelly Roll Morton
The Hot Five—Louis Armstrong
The Hot Seven—Louis Armstrong
Original Dixieland Jazz Band—Nick LaRocca
Georgia Jazz Band—Ma Rainey
Original Tuxedo Orchestra—Papa Celestin
Dixie Syncopators—King Oliver
The Wolverines—Bix Beiderbecke
Creole Jazz Band—Kid Ory
Superior Band—Bunk Johnson

Be able to identify the following items, places, and events that were involved in the development of jazz.

Chicago Exposition of 1893   polyrhythm
Amplivox   marching bands
Pianola   Vodun
secret societies   player piano
quadroon balls   first published rag
octaroon balls   ethnic music
Al Capone   Sedalia, Mo.
Pendergast Machine   Prohibition
speakeasies   Tivoli Ballroom
Black Codes   Union Ballroom
Clef Club   Underground Railroad
pit orchestra   Maple Leaf Club

Know the first two instrumental groups (bands—one black, one white) to make a recording, and the locations of the recording studios.

Know which jazz musicians to this point composed music for opera and symphony orchestras.

Study Guide for Final Examination

This study guide, together with that provided for the mid-term examination, will provide the student with a comprehensive review of the course material.

A portion of the final examination will be based on material found in the mid-term, which encompassed the eras of the Work Song, Ragtime, Minstrelsy, and Dixieland. The major part of the examination will focus on the eras of Tin Pan Alley, Swing/Big Bands, Be-Bop, Cool, and the beginning of Rock.

Tin Pan Alley

Know the location and the founder. Know the composers and the people and events for which they wrote, as well as the people associated with the era and the effect it had upon the continuing development of jazz.

Know the compositions which became standards in the repertoire of the performers in the eras that followed. Know the role of the singer as a result of this era.

Swing/Big Bands

Know the changes that took place from the Dixieland bands to the swing bands in relation to size, instrumentation, type of music, improvisation, location, and types of engagements.

In addition, be familiar with the following:

> The arrangers and their influence on the bands
> The influence of radio
> The influence of television
> Booking agencies
> The Musicians' Union
> Types of bands: hot, sweet, novelty, specialty
> Leaders, lead men, jazz men, sidemen
> The influence of the recording industry
> The meaning of territory, studio, road, location
> The places in which bands performed

Know the following bands:

Hot

Paul Whiteman	Cab Calloway	Buddy Rich
Duke Ellington	Harry James	Les Brown
Fletcher Henderson	Glenn Miller	Woody Herman
Count Basie	The Dorseys	Gene Krupa
Ben Pollack	(Jimmy-Tommy)	Erskine Hawkins
Benny Goodman	Stan Kenton	Chick Webb
Maynard Ferguson		

Sweet

Del Courtney	Freddie Martin	Ozzie Nelson
Lawrence Welk	Henry Busse	Jan Garber
Guy Lombardo	Tiny Hill	Dick Jurgens
Art Kassel	Sammy Kaye	Kay Kayser
Vaughn Monroe	Fred Waring	Rudy Vallee

Latin	*Novelty*	*Woman Bandleader*
Xavier Cugat	Spike Jones	Ina Rae Hutton

All Women Band

Phil Spitalny

Be-Bop

Know the reasons for the development of this era.
Know the location of the era's beginnings.
Know the leaders of the era and their particular musical abilities.
Know the types of places in which they performed.
Know the composers of the music.
Know the reasons for its demise.
Know the characteristics of the music.

Bop Artists:

Trumpet	*Sax*	*Trombone*	*Piano*
Dizzy Gillespie	Charlie Parker	Kai Winding	Thelonious Monk
Miles Davis	Stan Getz	Frank Rosolino	George Shearing
Howard McGhee	Zoot Sims	J. J. Johnson	Oscar Peterson
Red Rodney	Sonny Rollins	Bob Brookmeyer	Lennie Tristano
Clark Terry	Al Cohn		Bud Powell

Bass	*Drums*
Slam Stewart	Max Roach
Oscar Pettiford	Kenny Clarke
Ray Brown	Roy Haynes
Charlie Mingus	Chano Pozo

Cool

Know the reasons for the development of this period.
Know the location of the "Cool School."
Know the leaders of the movement.
Know the characteristics of the music.
Know the reason for its lack of popularity with the majority of the listening audience.
Know why it was called "Chamber Jazz."
Know which instruments were employed for the first time in jazz.

Cool (West Coast Jazz) Artists:

Trumpet	*Sax*	*Trombone*	*Piano*
Miles Davis	Paul Desmond	Bob Brookmeyer	Bill Evans
Chet Baker	Art Pepper	Frank Rosolino	Dave Brubeck
Jack Sheldon	Gerry Mulligan		Horace Silver
	John Coltrane		

Bass	*Drums*	*Composer/Arranger*
Paul Chambers	Shelly Manne	Paul Desmond—"Take Five"
Tommy Potter		Gil Evans—"Birth of the Cool," "Miles Ahead"
		Bill Evans—"Kinda Blue"
		Thelonious Monk—"Round Midnight"
		Dave Brubeck—"In Your Own Sweet Way"

Rock

Know when it began, why it began, and the performers who helped originate it.

Appendix B: Discography

Through all the eras of jazz beginning with ragtime and the first recordings of this new music, musicians have been identified by their best known works. Trivia, a word which has captivated society in recent years, has found its way into all phases and activities throughout the country. A fun game titled Trivial Pursuit was one of the most popular games in recent history, for a time replacing the traditional favorite, Monopoly. The spin-off of the trivia game created a curiosity in people of all ages as to who the best athletes were by their personal achievement records; best contemporary artists; the best photographers of people, nature, national events; the best actors, actresses, and the best movie of any given year.

Each year, music magazines such as *Downbeat*, *Metronome* and *Playboy*, as well as many of the specific trade journals (*Modern Drummer*) conduct polls to determine who the best musicians are for a particular year. The record industry likewise awards Grammys to the outstanding recording artists each year.

With this as a format, it was felt that while the artists listed in either a category or a decade were all prominent performers, it would be of interest to determine by which of their recordings they are best known.

Using professional musicians, teachers, and students as a population for a poll, the following recordings (not albums) were found to be those for which the artist is most remembered.

Ragtime:

Eubie Blake	Memories of You
Scott Joplin	Maple Leaf Rag
Huddie "Leadbelly" Ledbetter	Eagle Rock Rag
Jelly Roll Morton	King Porter Stomp
Fats Waller	Ain't Misbehavin'

Dixieland:

Louis Armstrong	Hello Dolly
Bix Beiderbecke	Swinging the Blues
Wingy Manone	Tailgate Ramble
King Oliver	West End Blues
Kid Ory	Muskrat Ramble

Big Bands

Charlie Barnett	Skyliner
Count Basie	April in Paris
Benny Berigan	I Can't Get Started
Les Brown	Sentimental Journey
Cab Calloway	Minnie the Moocher
Bob Crosby	Big Noise from Winnetka
Jimmy Dorsey	So Rare
Tommy Dorsey	Marie
Duke Ellington	Take the "A" Train
Maynard Ferguson	Gonna Fly Now
Benny Goodman	Stompin' at the Savoy
Glen Gray	Sunrise Serenade
Lionel Hampton	Flyin' Home

Fletcher Henderson	Nagasaki
Woody Herman	Woodchoppers Ball
Harry James	Ciribiribin
Stan Kenton	Artistry in Rhythm
Gene Krupa	Sing, Sing, Sing
Guy Lombardo	Auld Lang Syne
Glenn Miller	In the Mood
Buddy Rich	West Side Story
Artie Shaw	Begin the Beguine
Charlie Spivak	Stardreams
Paul Whiteman	Rhapsody in Blue

Be-Bop/Cool:

Art Blakey	Moanin'
Dave Brubeck	Take Five
John Coltrane	Naima
Miles Davis	'Round Midnight
Erroll Garner	Misty
Stan Getz	Early Autumn
Dizzey Gillespie	Night in Tunisia
Howard McGhee	Thermodynamics
Thelonious Monk	'Round Midnight
Wes Montgomery	Bumpin'
Charlie Parker	Ornithology
Oscar Peterson	Just Friends
Django Reinhardt	Crazy Rhythm
George Shearing	September in the Rain
Joe Venuti	After You've Gone

Singers:

Tony Bennett	I Left My Heart in San Francisco
Nat Cole	Unforgettable
Bing Crosby	White Christmas
Billy Eckstine	Caravan
Ella Fitzgerald	A Tiskit A Tasket
Judy Garland	Over the Rainbow
Billie Holliday	God Bless the Child
Lena Horne	Stormy Weather
Mahalia Jackson	Amazing Grace
Peggy Lee	Fever
Lizzie Miles	Bill Bailey
Liza Minnelli	New York, New York
Anita O'Day	Let Me Off Uptown
Frank Sinatra	My Way
Bessie Smith	Empty Bed Blues
Mamie Smith	That Thing Called Love
Barbra Streisand	The Way We Were
Jimmy Rushing	Harvard Blues
Mel Torme	The Christmas Song
Sarah Vaughn	Misty

| Dinah Washington | What A Difference a Day Makes |
| Joe Williams | Everyday |

Rock:

50's

Chuck Berry	Johnny B. Goode
Chubby Checker	The Twist
Elvis Presley	Jail House Rock, Hound Dog
Fats Domino	Blueberry Hill
Bill Haley & the Comets	Rock Around the Clock
Buddy Holly	Peggy Sue
Jerry Lee Lewis	Great Balls of Fire
Little Richard	Tutti Fruitti, Good Golly Miss Molly

60's

Beach Boys	Surfin' U.S.A.
Beatles	Hey, Jude, Yesterday
Four Tops	I'll Be There
Aretha Franklin	Respect
Grateful Dead	Truckin'
Janis Joplin	Me & Bobby McGee
Smokey Robinson	Tears of a Clown
Rolling Stones	Satisfaction
Supremes	Stop in the Name of Love
Temptations	My Girl
The Who	Talking 'bout my Generation

70's

Blood, Sweat & Tears	Spinning Wheel
David Bowie	Major Tom
Chicago	Saturday in the Park
The Doors	Light My Fire
Eagles	Hotel California
Genesis	ABACAB
Led Zeplin	Stairway to Heaven
Pink Floyd	Another Brick in the Wall
Bruce Springsteen	Born in the U.S.A.
Frank Zappa	Valley Girl

80's

| Squeeze | Black Coffee in Bed |
| U-2 | Sunday, Bloody Sunday |

American Folk Music

Alabama	Mountain Music
Chet Atkins	Certified Guitar Player
Joan Baez	Diamonds and Rust
Glen Campbell	Rhinestone Cowboy

Johnny Cash	I Walk the Line
Patsy Cline	Crazy
Judy Collins	Send in the Clowns
Crystal Gayle	Don't It Make My Brown Eyes Blue
Arlo Guthrie	Alice's Restaurant
Waylon Jennings	Luckenback, Texas
Loretta Lynn	Coal Miner's Daughter
Willie Nelson	On the Road Again
Nitty Gritty Dirt Band	Mr. Bojangles
Oakridge Boys	Elvira
Dolly Parton	Nine to Five
Peter, Paul & Mary	Puff the Magic Dragon
Charlie Pride	Behind Closed Doors
Kenny Rogers	Lady, The Gambler
George Strait	Amarillo by Morning
Hank Williams Sr.	Your Cheatin' Heart
Tammy Wynette	Stand by Your Man

Appendix C: Sample Examination Questions

As an assist to the student of jazz history, following are a number of questions usually asked on examinations. Since this is merely a sampling of the various eras of jazz, the student can mentally expand and encompass the whole history of jazz up through the beginning of the rock era. The questions have been structured in several forms from essay to true-false to multiple choice and matching.

1. Trace the chronological development of jazz from its beginnings in America to the beginnings of the rock era.

2. List several leading exponents of jazz from each era beginning with minstrelsy through the beginnings of rock and describe their particular contributions.

3. What are the principal characteristics that each era derived from its predecessor?

4. What effect did labor organizations have on the development of jazz?

5. During which era did racial discrimination have an effect on the development of jazz?

6. During which era did Europe get involved with jazz and begin supporting same?

7. What is meant by the term "The Spanish Tinge"?

8. What effect did the Spanish Tinge have on the development of jazz?

9. The structure of early jazz found during ragtime and Dixieland came from another musical media. What was that media and how did it affect jazz?

10. A number of jazz musicians past and present encompassed several eras of jazz throughout their careers. Name ten of them and list their inclusive eras.

11. Name the different types of bands found during the big band era and describe their differences relative to size, style, type of music performed, locales in which they performed and geographic territory in which they toured.

12. Describe the functions of a booking agency as relates to the music industry.

13. Where was the location of Tin Pan Alley and what activity took place there?

14. What was the musical difference between the Bop and Cool eras? When were they active in jazz history? What were the reasons for their birth and death?

15. What influence did the Austin High Gang have on the development of jazz?

16. Describe the difference between New Orleans style Dixieland and Chicago style Dixieland.

17. Describe the difference that took place in the transition from the style of Dixieland to that of the swing/big band era.

18. Describe the role of women in the development of jazz.

19. List the staffing of a big band of eighteen players from sideman to leader. Describe the role of each member.

20. What was the role of singers during the big band era?

21. What effect did movies and radio have on the development of jazz?

22. How did the recording industry help or deter the development of jazz?

23. What factors play an important role in the development of a specific era of jazz.

True–False

1. MCA, the Music Corporation of America, became one of the major publishing firms as a result of the large volume of music produced in Tin Pan Alley.

2. "Stoptime" was a background effect sometimes used as a backup for an instrumental or vocal solo.

3. A "tag" ending to a composition was added after the selection had been played/sung through the original chorus.

4. A jam session at which various bands or individuals tried to outplay each other was called a "cutting contest."

5. New meters such as 5/4 and 9/4 were utilized in the "bop" era.

6. The sax playing arranger on the Louis Armstrong big band was Don Redman.

7. A head arrangement is one which is memorized by all the members of the band.

8. The Charleston was a popular dance during the ragtime era.

9. George Gershwin is credited with being the founder of Tin Pan Alley.

10. Double entendre as related to jazz history was first used in the lyrics of the songs about slavery sung in various minstrel shows.

11. Bing Crosby, having received his start as a singer with Paul Whiteman, was really catapulted to fame by writing and singing his best known song, "White Christmas."

12. In the blues chord progression, the I chord is used for a total of eight measures.

Multiple Choice

1. The saxophonist who encompassed all the periods of jazz including minstrel shows, big bands, bop, cool, Dixieland was
   a. John Coltrane
   b. Coleman Hawkins
   c. Lester Young
   d. Zoot Sims

2. A composer who wrote much of the material used in minstrel shows was
   a. Stephen Foster
   b. Victor Herbert
   c. Irving Berlin
   d. George Gershwin

3. Which of the following components in music is more essential in classical music?
   a. melody
   b. harmony
   c. countermelody
   d. rhythm

4. Double entendre was
   a. playing a part of a composition in double time (twice as fast)
   b. playing the bridge of a tune in double time
   c. double meaning for a word or expression
   d. doubling the number of players on a part

5. Which of the following cities contributed least to the development of jazz?
   a. Memphis
   b. New York
   c. Chicago
   d. New Orleans

6. Which of the following men claimed to be the "inventor of jazz"?
   a. Scott Joplin
   b. Tom Turpin
   c. Jelly Roll Morton
   d. Paul Whiteman

7. Which man is the first to develop and achieve fame as a big band leader?
   a. Benny Moten
   b. Fletcher Henderson
   c. Benny Goodman
   d. Count Basie

8. The rock era was ushered in by,
   a. The Beatles
   b. Chicago
   c. Bill Haley & the Comets
   d. Blood, Sweat & Tears

9. Don Redman was the arranger for which one of the following big bands?
   a. Duke Ellington
   b. Harry James
   c. Fletcher Henderson
   d. Cab Calloway

10. The first black band to do a professional recording was,
    a. Duke Ellington
    b. The Hot Seven
    c. Kid Ory
    d. The Red Hot Peppers

11. Which bandleader is credited with playing the first "jazz concert"?
    a. Paul Whiteman
    b. Jelly Roll Morton
    c. Louis Armstrong
    d. Benny Goodman

12. Which bandleader is credited with racially integrating his band via a featured quartet?
    a. Stan Kenton
    b. The Dorsey Brothers
    c. Duke Ellington
    d. Benny Goodman

Matching

Match the person, event, title, dance, with a specific era.

a. work song

b. minstrelsy

c. ragtime

d. Dixieland

e. Tin Pan Alley

1. Pit orchestra B

2. Follow the Drinkin' Gourd A

3. Mr. Bones B

4. Tom Turpin C

5. Cakewalk A

6. Lindy Hop D

7. Harry Von Tilzer E

8. Interlocutor B

9. Early Gospel Music A

10. The Hot Five D

11. The Brill Building E

12. The tack piano D

13. Maple Leaf Club C

14. Richard Rodgers D

15. Piano rolls C

16. Song pluggers C

The big bands added singers to their organizations. Match a singer with a particular band with which he/she sang.

Singer

a.	Count Basie	17. June Christy	d
b	Benny Goodman	18. Billie Holliday	a
c	Harry James	19. Frank Sinatra	c
d.	Stan Kenton	20. Helen Forrest	b
e.	Paul Whiteman	21. Bing Crosby	e

Some of the big bands had vocal groups attached as part of the band. Match a group with a band.

Vocal Group

a.	Paul Whiteman	22. The Modernaires	d
b.	Tommy Dorsey	23. The Moonmaids	c
c.	Vaughn Monroe	24. The Rhythm Boys	a
d.	Glenn Miller	25. The Pied Pipers	b

Match The Following People Into Songwriting Teams

a.	George Gershwin	26. Lorenz Hart	b
b.	Richard Rodgers	27. Walter Donaldson	c
c.	Gus Kahn	28. Harold Arlen	d
d.	Johnny Mercer	29. Ira Gershwin	a
e.	Jerome Kern	30. Otto Harbach	e

Index

114